# Inspiring Women

# Finding freedom

## The joy of surrender

**Helena Wilkinson**

Copyright © CWR 2007

Published 2007 by CWR, Waverley Abbey House, Waverley Lane, Farnham, Surrey GU9 8EP, UK.

The right of Helena Wilkinson to be identified as the author of this work has been asserted by her in accordance with the Copyright, Designs and Patents Act 1988, sections 77 and 78.

See back of book for list of National Distributors.

Unless otherwise indicated, all Scripture references are from the Holy Bible: New International Version (NIV), copyright © 1973, 1978, 1984 by the International Bible Society. Other versions marked: Amp: The Amplified Bible © 1987 Zondervan and the Lockwood Foundation. CEV: Contemporary English Version © 1995 by American Bible Society. GNB: Good News Bible, © 1996,1971,1976, American Bible Society. GWT: God's Word translation © God's Word to the Nations. NASB: New American Standard Bible, © 1977, Lockman Corporation. NLT: New Living Translation © 1996. Phillips: J.B. Phillips, The New Testament in Modern English, © 1960,1972, J.B. Phillips, Fount Paperbacks.

Concept development, editing, design and production by CWR

Cover image: Jupiterimages/Workbook Stock

Printed in Finland by WS Bookwell

ISBN: 978-1-85345-451-6

# Contents

# Introduction

The greatness of man's power is in the measure of his surrender.

William Booth

A couple of years ago Sue, now one of my closest friends, burst through the door with bundles of enthusiasm. She had stumbled across a rather tatty, old red hardback book. The book was *Kept for the Master's Use*, written by Frances Ridley Havergal in 1879.

'I'm discovering what it means to say to God, "Take my days, my hours, my moments", she said, 'and it's incredible.'

I was captivated by Sue's passion for the book and weeks later enquired how she was getting on. She was still on the same chapter and I was puzzled as to why it was taking her so long. However, as I was to find out for myself, to hand over areas of your life and to follow through on what you offer to God, is *not* a quick process. Just as Frances Ridley Havergal had pored over each word she wrote in expounding on what it means to say, 'Take my life, and let it be/Consecrated, Lord, to Thee!', so Sue was being confronted and changed by each word she read.

There was a lightness developing in Sue's life as she no longer regarded her time, finances, possessions, work and activities as her own. I, on the other hand, worried about many things, and time and circumstances too often controlled me. The thought of following in Sue's footsteps felt like hard work, but nonetheless I decided to tackle the subject of surrender for CWR's devotional *Inspiring Women Every Day*.

Initially I thought of entitling the Bible notes *The Challenge of Surrender*, for surrender is, without doubt, a challenge, but the word 'challenge' didn't sit right. I found myself drawn to the word 'joy' and called the notes *The Joy of Surrender*, knowing that if only we can get past the effort and pain of surrender, then we can encounter the deepest joy.

The Bible notes impacted many people's lives and as a result it was decided that I take the theme a little further and write a book. As is often the case with devotional writers, my developing the theme required a personal journey. The longer I travelled on that journey (which essentially involved walking further down the path of surrender than I had ever done) the more I discovered that it was, in fact, a journey about finding freedom.

The paths you walk along as you read this book may not always be easy, but I pray that God will bless you in the reading as much as He has blessed me in the writing. I pray too that as you surrender old and new areas of your life it will open the door for other people to surrender more of their lives, and that they, like you, will reap the rewards.

Helena Wilkinson, Gower, Swansea, 2007

## Chapter 1

# Embrace surrender

'Trust in the LORD with all your heart
and lean not on your own understanding;
in all your ways acknowledge him,
and he will make your paths straight.'
Proverbs 3:5–6

I was just about to leave a friend's house recently when he turned to me and said, 'Did you see what I got Angus for Christmas?' With that, Philip picked up a remote control and pointed it at a toy police Land Rover which shot across the wooden floor at high speed, sirens blaring and doors flying open.

Philip was simply showing me how his eight-year-old son's present worked, but imagine if he were always the one who controlled the operating of it. The toy would have been *given* but not *given over*. I wonder if we do similarly with God – give our lives to Him, yet not give over *all* aspects of our lives.

We sing, 'I surrender all, all to Thee, my blessed Saviour, I surrender all'[1], but do we? If we are to find freedom in all areas of our lives then, I believe, we must move from simply *following* Jesus to *living for* Jesus. To do that requires us to *embrace surrender*. It is only in surrender that we encounter satisfaction irrespective of circumstance.

The trouble is that surrender has negative connotations and we have a tendency to shy away from it as we ponder the effort required and the price to be paid. What if we have to give up things that we don't want to give up; what about the fact that surrender is associated with being defeated? We live in a competitive society and, as Rick Warren points out, 'If winning is everything, surrender is *unthinkable*. We would rather talk about winning, succeeding, overcoming, and conquering than yielding, submitting, obeying, and surrendering.'[2]

In order to surrender we must be convinced that surrender is positive, not negative, and we must rid ourselves of the viewpoint that it is a sign of weakness. Paul reminds us in 2 Corinthians: 'For when I am weak, then I am strong' (12:10). Only when we are weak are we dependent on God's grace:

'… My grace is sufficient for you, for my power is made perfect in weakness' (12:9).

## What does surrender mean?

The dictionary definition of surrender is to relinquish possession or control to another; to give up in favour of another; to give up or give back (that which has been granted); to abandon; to give over or resign (oneself) to something.[3] Other words used to describe surrender include: yield, let go (of), deliver (up), forsake, turn over, part with, comply, concede, give (oneself) up. The word refers to submission, renunciation, relinquishment and transferral.[4]

Surrender, in biblical terms, means that we become fully God's and not our own. It is about allowing *our* desires to be brought in line with *God's* desires. Many times in my life people have given me a word which has included the verse from Psalm 37:4: 'Delight yourself in the Lord and he will give you the desires of your heart.' On more than one occasion I have been convinced that I *had* taken delight in the Lord and yet what I longed for still evaded me. I was puzzled over why I never seemed to see the fruit. Then one day I realised several things:

1. There is a difference between *wants* and *desires*: wants have to do with longings focused on self; desires are from the heart and are in conjunction with vision or destiny.
2. We are most likely to see the fulfilment of our desires when they match God's desires.
3. The *granting* of our desires begins with the *surrender* of our desires. (Verse 5 of Psalm 37 says: 'Commit your way to the Lord; trust in him and he will do this …')

Commit means to entrust or consign for safekeeping[5] or to place in trust or charge.[6] Do you entrust all areas of your life into the safe-keeping of God's hands and trust Him to be in charge, or do you try to take charge yourself and hold on to the control of some areas?

## God's agenda or mine?

I have begun to see that without my ways continually surrendered to God, my desires are unlikely to be the same as His. Rather than praying that God will grant me my heart's desires, I now tend to pray that God will show me what His desires are and that mine will come in line with His. Leading up to praying that way I had to ask myself, 'Do I hold in my mind God's agenda for my life or my own agenda? Do I want God's desires and plans or am I trying to twist His arm to give me my fleshly wants?'

The turning point for me was a reading in *The Word For Today*,[7] where the author writes: 'Do not ask God to bless your plans, ask Him to show you His; they are already blessed. When the time is right the plan will be clear, the people in place and the resources available.' There is a distinct difference in how things work out when we are flowing with God's plans rather than endeavouring to swim against the tide in an effort to maintain our own.

To surrender and allow God to be Lord of our lives involves not only a letting go but a belief that God directs our lives. Do you consider that life 'just happens' or that God is actually in control? What about when, in your eyes, things 'go wrong'? To believe that God is in control means riding the storm when life is uncomfortable and holding on to the truth that '… in all things God works for the good of those who love him, who have been called according to his purpose' (Rom. 8:28). 'Works for the good' does not necessarily mean that things work out well; essentially it refers to that which conforms to the likeness of God's Son, so, in all things, however difficult, God works in our lives to bring about the likeness of Jesus in us.

We can so easily make the assumption that if we love God and trust Him then our lives will be free from trouble, but in thinking like this we actually miss the point. *We* tend to be interested in our *good* and our *happiness* but *God's* interest is our *moulding, shaping* and *conformity to the characteristics of His Son.*

C.S. Lewis once said, 'The more we let God take us over, the more truly ourselves we become – because he made us.' Embracing surrender, and discovering the joy of surrender, is about allowing God to take our lives, thus enabling us to become the people He intends us to be. Not only do we become the people God intends us to be, but the more closely we walk with God the more we reflect His character.

## Self-examination

To embrace surrender means examining our walk with God on a regular basis and no longer compartmentalising our lives: that is, following God's way in one area of our lives and our own way in another! It is easy to give certain parts of ourselves and our lives to God whilst holding others back because we are wrestling with the need to be in control. A.W. Tozer once said, 'The reason why many are still troubled, still seeking, still making little forward progress is because they haven't yet come to the end of themselves. We're still trying to give orders, and interfering with God's work within us.'

What is it in us that causes us to interfere with God's work? Is it doubt that God will meet our deepest needs or horror at the thought of not being the one in control? Rick Warren believes that 'There are three barriers that block our total surrender to God: fear, pride, and confusion.'[8] Before we go any further, can you take the different areas to be addressed in this book (heart, will, mind, body, time, words, love, worship) and ask yourself if there is a barrier to your surrendering any of these aspects, and if so what the barrier is and why it exists?

I have often found that the times I have been most willing to surrender, and have grown the most in my relationship with God, are when my life has fallen to pieces and I can no longer be in control. I liken it to dying, that has to take place prior to resurrection being possible. When I was living in rural Southern Africa, at some point during the winter the veldt (open land) would be set on fire. To anyone passing by the land looked dead and wasted; rather like dense black treacle through which nothing would ever emerge. However, with the first few drops of rain, bright green shoots would push their way through the blackness and out of nowhere new life would spring forth. In the same way, surrender involves a coming to the end of ourselves; letting that which is of ourselves die, in order that God-breathed life can emerge in us and bear fruit.

The dying process involves letting go and the truth is that many of us find it hard to let go because underneath we fear that God might not step in. Even if we do believe He will step in, there is often a fear that He will give us less than best or turn our life into something that we don't want.

When we encounter doubts about whether God has in mind the best for us, it is good to remind ourselves of God's intervention with Jesus. In His humanity Jesus did not want the cup of suffering which was before Him in the Garden of Gethsemane, but nevertheless He trusted His Father, surrendered His will and, as a result, God brought into being the incredible plan of salvation. When we trust God and surrender to Him, He brings about His best for our lives (though we rarely see the full fruit until we look back).

## Relationship and obedience

Jesus surrendered in response to His *relationship* with His Father and in *obedience* to Him; in the same way our choice to surrender must grow out of a *relationship* of love and a *willingness* to obey. True surrender is based on complete confidence in the one to whom we surrender; and it involves yielding ourselves to the one in whom we have put our trust. We are not going to surrender to anyone in whom we do not have confidence. Do you have confidence in God? Do you trust Him? Trust means a firm belief in the reliability, truth or strength of a person … a confident expectation.[9] It involves a firm reliance on the integrity, ability or character of a person. Do you see God as fulfilling these?

We can have trust in the:
- everlasting strength of God – '… the LORD, is the Rock eternal' (Isa. 26:4)
- goodness of God – 'For the LORD is good and his love endures for ever …' (Psa. 100:5)
- loving-kindness of God – 'How priceless is your unfailing love! …' (Psa. 36:7)
- bounty of God – '… God, who richly provides us with everything for our enjoyment' (1 Tim. 6:17)
- care of God for us – 'Cast all your anxiety on him because he cares for you' (1 Pet. 5:7)
- fact that He won't forsake us – '… for you, LORD, have never forsaken those who seek you' (Psa. 9:10).

Our trust in God leads to:

- the enjoyment of perfect peace (Isa. 26:3)
- our prospering and being blessed (Prov. 16:20)
- rejoicing in Him (Psa. 5:11; 33:21)
- the fulfilment of the desires of our hearts (Psa. 37:4)
- deliverance from enemies (Psa. 37:40)
- safety in times of danger (Prov. 29:25)
- stability and security (Prov. 18:10).

Putting our confidence and trust in God and surrendering our lives to Him will bring greater fruitfulness. It may not always be comfortable but surrender will ultimately result in maturity, Christ-likeness and holiness.

## For reflection

### Scriptures

*'for it is God who works in you to will and to act according to his good purpose.'* (Phil. 2:13)

*'Direct me in the path of your commands, for there I find delight. Turn my heart towards your statutes and not towards selfish gain.'* (Psa. 119:35–36)

### Thought

We need to examine our motives before making a choice to surrender.

### Action

What aspects of your life do you feel are yet to be surrendered? Can you talk to God about what holds you back from surrendering these areas and choose to relinquish control?

### Prayer

*Lord Jesus, You laid down Your life for me and I don't ever want to take it for granted. Help me to surrender more of my life to You. I lay down my own agenda, plans and ideas and choose to trust You and seek Your will for my life. Thank You that there is no safer place than my life in Your hands. Amen.*

**Chapter 2**

# Soften your heart

*'Create in me a pure heart, O God, and renew
a steadfast spirit within me'*
Psalm 51:10

When you consider your walk with God do you ever feel a hypocrite – a mixture of a godly and an ungodly person? Do you, at times, feel as though the impression that others have of you and how you feel on the inside are very different? There's a wonderful little poem by Edward Sanford Martin which sums up these thoughts:

> Within my earthly temple, there's a crowd;
> There's one of us that's humble, one that's proud;
> There's one that's broken-hearted for his sins;
> There's one that, unrepentant, sits and grins;
> There's one that loves his neighbour as himself,
> And one that cares for naught but fame and self.
> From much corroding care I should be free
> If I could once determine which is me.[1]

## Searching and understanding

In our natural selves, and without walking the path of surrender, our lives can be quite mixed up. I remember hearing someone say, 'We all surrender to something; it's just a question of what we surrender to.' E. Stanley Jones took this a little further when he said (as quoted in Rick Warren's *Purpose Driven Life*), 'If you don't surrender to Christ, you surrender to chaos.' There is no doubt that an un-surrendered heart can lead to internal and external chaos. Anger, resentment, jealousy, distorted thinking and a broken relationship with others and with God can be some of the consequences.

When we use the word un-surrendered we may hold in our mind someone who is hardened to the gospel. Is that really so? What does an un-surrendered heart mean? Is it someone who has not given their life to Jesus or could it be someone who has given their life to Him but not *given over* their heart and all that is within it? Is it not true that we can give our life to Jesus but withhold a part of our heart, thus short-changing Him?

We may genuinely love the Lord and yet, to our shame, still have ungodly attitudes and actions. We need to remind ourselves that to walk with the Lord (rather than simply acknowledge who He is or declare that we love Him) is to *continually* ask Him to reveal all that is within us which is not honouring to Him. David asks God, 'Search me, O God, and know my heart; test me and know my anxious thoughts' (Psa. 139:23). And he tells his son, Solomon, '… acknowledge the God of your father, and serve him with wholehearted devotion and with a willing mind, for the LORD searches every heart and understands every motive behind the thoughts …' (1 Chron. 28:9) How often do you ask God to search *your* heart? Would you feel threatened or apprehensive about doing so, or would you welcome His highlighting anything that needs to be addressed?

When we ask God to search our hearts we come to realise that they are not always very nice. Jeremiah, a priest with a prophetic ministry during the days of King Solomon, makes this clear when he declares that: 'The heart is deceitful above all things …' (Jer. 17:9) His words are as relevant today as they were in King Solomon's time. Besides being corrupt (Psa. 14:1) and deceitful (Jer. 17:9), Scripture reveals to us that our hearts are also naturally sinful (Heb. 3:12), weak-willed (Ezek. 16:30), double-minded (Psa. 12:2), rebellious (Jer. 5:23), hard and obstinate (Ezek. 3:7), stony (Ezek. 11:19), proud (Prov. 21:4), perverse (Prov. 17:20), foolish (Rom. 1:21).

## Softening and remoulding

King David is a good example of someone whose heart was for God and yet, like so many of us, it led him into thought and behaviour patterns that were against God's principles. The corruption in his heart resulted in both adultery and murder.

It is often when we are at our lowest ebb and faced with our gravest mistakes, as was David, that we are most open to God challenging, softening and remoulding our hearts, but we still have a choice over whether we allow God to work in this way. In Psalm 86, we see that David made this choice when he prayed, 'Teach me your way, O LORD, and I will walk in your truth; give me an undivided heart, that I may fear your name' (Psa. 86:11).

In Psalm 51, David recognises the results of his deceitful heart and cries out to God to change it: 'Create in me a clean heart, O God, And renew a steadfast spirit within me' (Psa. 51:10, NASB). This is one of the most powerful passages in the Bible concerning a changed heart. David recognised his wrongdoing. His repentance involved godly sorrow, verbal confession, turning from sin, forgiveness, restoration to God's favour, rejoicing in salvation and the desire to testify to others about God's grace. This enabled him to move from a place of deceit to a place of integrity. Integrity is moral uprightness, honesty, wholeness, soundness.[2] It involves strict adherence to a code of moral values ... and complete sincerity or honesty.[3]

No doubt David desired such integrity when he asked God to create in him a clean heart. The Hebrew word used for 'create' indicates an activity that can be performed *only* by God. Amongst other things it means to engrave and carve. I have a friend who is a sculptor and when he engraves or carves his stone, his work is permanent. In the same way, the work that God does in our hearts has permanency about it. The

Hebrew for 'clean heart' means a purified heart and occurs ninety-four times in the Hebrew Old Testament, indicating its importance.

## God's heart for us

In order to soften and change our hearts we need to a) see God's heart for us and b) draw aside in order that He can change our hearts.

God's heart is a heart of love. One image of His love for us is as a shepherd. Jesus said, 'I am the good shepherd. The good shepherd lays down his life for his sheep' (John 10:11). I see gentleness in God's heart as He holds us as vulnerable lambs against His chest. 'He tends his flock like a shepherd: He gathers the lambs in his arms and carries them close to his heart; he gently leads those that have young' (Isa. 40:11). His heart beats rhythmically with life, and radiates warmth and protection. His love is strong, bright, fruitful, energising and all-embracing.

His heart is also a covenantal heart. He makes and keeps promises. His commitment to us as His children is constantly portrayed throughout Scripture. One of my favourite readings is God's promise to Joshua after Moses' death. Joshua was getting the people ready to cross the Jordan River into the promised land. God said, 'As I was with Moses, so I will be with you; I will never leave you nor forsake you' (Josh. 1:5). Because the Lord will never leave him nor forsake him, Joshua is instructed to be strong and courageous and not to be terrified or discouraged (Josh. 1:9).

Once we know God's heart for us it becomes easier to draw aside and allow Him to work on *our* hearts. We need to find a place of solitude and quiet where there is only God with whom we can connect, open up and pour out our hearts: a place where our hearts can meet with the heart of God. Withdrawal is often necessary because of the distraction of the world and, depending on our circumstances, the place and length of time will vary. Quality is the all-important element. Although Jesus was always listening to His Father, He had times when He drew aside from the crowd, taking Himself to a quiet place up a mountain. No doubt these moments were far more intimate than His everyday interaction with His Father. Where is your place of rest?

In our time of drawing aside it is helpful to look at whether there is any resistance in us to giving God the whole of our hearts and allowing Him to shape them. The heart, for many, can feel vulnerable (because it is the part of ourselves that we tend to want to protect), so unless we take the risk and trust God it is easy to hold back from fully surrendering ourselves to Him. Can you talk to God about *your* vulnerabilities and ask Him to help shape your heart into one that reflects His?

## Changed and transformed

When our hearts have been softened and are malleable, the process of change becomes quicker and easier and we are more able to surrender the different areas of our lives.

In the book of Ezekiel, after the judgment on Israel's leaders, there is the promised return of Israel where God says that He will gather the Israelites from the nations and bring them back from the countries in which they have been scattered. But this is not all; God also declares, 'I will give them an undivided heart and put a new spirit in them; I will remove from them their heart of stone and give them a heart of flesh' (Ezek. 11:19). This is so significant for us as we journey into deeper places with God and give Him more of ourselves. What is being spoken of here is an inner spiritual and moral transformation that results in single-minded commitment to the Lord and to His will. Ezekiel 11:20 goes on to speak of the results of such a change of heart: 'Then they will follow my decrees and be careful to keep my laws.' A heart of flesh; a heart surrendered by us and transformed by the Lord, enables us to conduct our lives in a way pleasing to Him.

Without God's hand upon us, we have the potential to lead very destructive lives. If we want to find freedom, we need to accept the state of our hearts. We must be prepared to address the corruption, however subtle that may be, because it affects so many aspects of us (the heart being the centre of our selves which includes our will, mind and emotions).

With God's hand upon our lives, Scripture tells us that God can make our hearts: pure (Psa. 51:10), good and noble (Luke 8:15), faithful (Neh. 9:8), discerning (1 Kings 3:9), contrite (Psa. 51:17), sincere (Heb. 10:22), glad (Psa. 16:9), wise (1 Kings 3:12), cheerful (Prov 17:22), steadfast and trusting (Psa. 112:7). And more! Oh, that our hearts would be like this at all times. It is only going to happen if we keep close to God and ask for His protection from the influences of the world, the flesh and the devil.

## For reflection

. . . . . . . . . . . . . . . . . . . . . . . . . . . . . . . . . . . . . . . . . . . . . . . .

### Scriptures

*'A heart at peace gives life to the body ...'* (Prov. 14:30)

*'Listen, my son, and be wise, and keep your heart on the right path.'* (Prov. 23:19)

### Thought

It is not worth covering up wrongness of heart, because just as light on a window shows up dirt, so the light of the Holy Spirit will show up any inconsistency or deceit in our lives.

### Action

Compare your heart with the list of scriptures in the section 'Searching and understanding' and with the last paragraph of this chapter. Can you bring before God what you would like to see change?

### Prayer

*Lord, I offer you the state of my heart and ask that You begin a softening and cleansing process so that I become more open to surrendering all aspects of my life to You. Amen.*

## Chapter 3

# Relinquish your will

*'If anyone would come after me, he must deny himself
and take up his cross and follow me.'*
Matthew 16:24

Toddlers and teenagers seem to have one characteristic in common – a battle of the will! Toddlers push the boundaries and teenagers make a bid for independence, although sometimes it is the reverse and all too often both are evident. As believers we are not dissimilar to them with our tendency to stubbornly follow the way of Adam and Eve in independent decision-making, signifying a battle for *our* will over *God's* will. Jeremiah summarises this in his words 'My people have committed two sins: They have forsaken me, the spring of living water, and have dug their own cisterns, broken cisterns that cannot hold water' (Jer. 2:13).

## Pulled in our own direction

We cry out to God for His guidance yet something within pulls us in our own direction. When we pray, we say how we long to do what God wants, but in our minds we easily hold on to an image of what *we* want, projecting this on to God. There is something in most of us that wants to hold on – hold on to what we have, what we know, what is predictable and how we envisage our lives could be.

In contrast to our natural instinct to hold on to self, Jesus teaches us about *laying self down*: 'If anyone would come after me, he must deny himself and take up his cross and follow me. For whoever wants to save his life will lose it, but whoever loses his life for me will find it' (Matt. 16:24–25). To lose our life requires us to let go of hindrances, the greatest of which, as Rick Warren points out, is ourselves: our 'self-will, stubborn pride, and personal ambition. You cannot fulfill God's purposes for your life while focusing on your own plans.'[1]

The danger is that if we do not surrender our will but go on choosing our own way we end up battling with the consequences of our independence. I remember a friend once telling me how she pleaded with God for her will in the area of ministry. When it later cost her her marriage, she had a sinking feeling that God had given her what she wanted but wondered if it had been His best for her.

This concept of God allowing us to have our desires (even if not the best for us) is echoed in C.S. Lewis's words: 'There are two kinds of people: those who say to God "Thy will be done" and those to whom God says "All right then, have it your way"'. Ever since listening to my friend and reading these words of C.S. Lewis, I find myself being honest with God about my desires but also telling Him that I only want them granted if they are His best for my life. I would rather be within God's will than simply have my own way. My guess is that having picked up this book there is also something in you that desires the will of God over and above your will?

## Relinquishing our rights

Even if it is our desire to follow God's will, it does not mean that we will find it easy or that there won't be an inner battle. We fight both the flesh and the enemy. Paul speaks openly of the battle between the spiritual and the unspiritual in his letter to the Romans: 'So I find this law at work: When I want to do good, evil is right there with me. For in my inner being I delight in God's law; but I see another law at work in the members of my body, waging war against the law of my mind and making me a prisoner of the law of sin at work within my members' (Rom. 7:21–23). Paul is talking of the law of sin, but the same law is at work in keeping us focused on, and trusting in, *our* will rather than *God's* will.

For most of us, surrendering our will is very much a process and the starting point is our relationship with God. We can't be nominal Christians and surrender our will. We need to be in love! It's not too late to move into a depth of relationship that says, 'I will follow you wherever you lead.' As humans we long to please and honour the person/people we love and are willing to make sacrifices concerning our own desires. To surrender our will to God means loving Him and being prepared to let go and allow our will to be shaped by Him.

Even when we have a deep relationship with the Lord, surrendering our will can often be preceded by a coming to terms with the death of our own will and perhaps a time of grief and even disappointment. This is something that I've recently gone through as I face the fact that my will (and what I hoped for, believed in and even thought at one stage was God's will) has not, as yet, come to fruition. I have had to face the fact that the ideal I held for my life may have been more about *my longings* than *God's best* for me. In my heart and mind I want God's will for my life above all else, but in conjunction with my emotions and my needs I have another picture.

The coming to terms with the fact that God may have a plan that is not in line with our longings is acutely painful. We may encounter disappointment as we go through the process of surrender, but when we do let go and fully enter into God's will we cannot be disappointed, for His ways are always higher than our ways (Isa. 55:9). The painful time is in the *letting go* of our will before we have seen the full picture of His will.

The choice to let go is not one that we make lightly; Frances Ridley Havergal in her hymn, 'Take My Life', makes it very clear that in surrendering her will, she is relinquishing her rights to own it:

> Take my will and make it Thine;
> It shall be no longer mine.

The thought of relinquishing all rights to our will can be frightening but again we must remember to whom we are relinquishing. God can do more with our lives than we could ever attempt, so is it not better to trust Him with His plans? 'Now to him who is able to do immeasurably more than all we ask or imagine, according to his power that is at work within us' (Eph. 3:20). To surrender our will and follow God's will results in our attaining our potential.

Relinquishing our rights to our will has an impact on other areas of our lives too. When we relinquish our rights we let go of ownership and this has the potential to be carried into such things as possessions. The only reason we can hold lightly to what is ours is because our eyes are opened to the fact that all that we have comes from God and we are merely the current stewards. What is God's is to be shared. This doesn't necessarily mean that we give all we have away but rather that we let go of materialism. What if God calls us to give something in our safekeeping to another; are we able to do so?

If we have surrendered our will and this has impacted the ownership of our possessions then we have a freedom to bless others in ways that perhaps we would not otherwise have been able to do. Like all aspects of surrender, the letting go of our rights to possessions and finance is a process; and as with all other areas of surrender, change in one area allows change in another and so the chain of surrender continues.

## Trusting God's plan

Surrendering our wills involves trusting God to bring about His plan for our lives. When we believe that God's will is so much better than ours it becomes easier to surrender to Him. Do you trust God? We need to remind ourselves that we have a

God who loves us and does not want to withhold good things from us. In the book of Matthew, Jesus said, 'Which of you, if his son asks for bread, will give him a stone? Or if he asks for a fish, will give him a snake? If you then, though you are evil, know how to give good gifts to your children, how much more will your Father in heaven give good gifts to those who ask him!' (Matt. 7:9–10) God delights to give us what we ask when it is within His will. He's not out to do the opposite of what we want; He longs to bless us in fulfilling His will for our lives even if at present we are puzzled over its outworking.

In the times when following God's will is more difficult, or we have been waiting and wondering what His plan is for us, it is good to keep our eyes focused on God and not on our situations, as challenging as this may be, and say with the psalmist, 'You have made known to me the path of life; you will fill me with joy in your presence …' (Psa. 16:11)

We also need to remind ourselves that surrender is a *giving over*, not a *giving up*. If we give up, we drown; if we give over, we move on. Maybe you know the story of the two frogs that fell into a bucket of cream. They both attempted to get out and failed. One gave up and drowned whilst the other persevered and paddled. He didn't give up and soon he found something solid under his feet and he hopped out. The cream had turned to butter. As we surrender and let God lead us, He turns things around for us in a way we cannot do.

## Time of waiting

Even when we have reached a place of trusting God it may be that we do not immediately know or see the fulfilment of His plans, as often there is a period of waiting. Many of us do not find waiting and being patient easy because when we have a plan we have the tendency to want to carry it out immediately. The first part of Psalm 37:7 reminds us, 'Surrender yourself to the LORD, and wait patiently for him' (GWT). To surrender is to be still, to be quiet, to put our confidence in God and to trust Him to bring about His plans for what it is we are seeking from Him.

The Bible is full of people who waited and who in the process had to trust God. Zechariah and Elizabeth waited for a child and despite her being barren she gave birth to John the Baptist. Simeon and Anna both waited a long time to see the Messiah, Simeon having been given a special insight by the Spirit in order that he would recognise the Christ. At the age of seventy-five, Abraham was given the promise by God, 'I will make you into a great nation' (Gen. 12:2–4), but as year after year passed by, he questioned how this could be so without a son. God appeared and spoke to him again when he was ninety-nine (Gen. 17:1) and Abraham asked, 'Will a son be born to a man a hundred years old?' (Gen. 17:17) God reassured him that this time next year his wife Sarah would have a son (Gen. 18:10). He had waited twenty-five years from the time of the initial promise to the time that Isaac was born. These and many other Bible characters waited but it wasn't simply a passive waiting; they actively sought the Lord.

What do you tend to do whilst you wait? Do you keep finding solutions and alternatives for God, keep reminding Him that He hasn't yet come up with the goods, or do you trust Him and thank Him that He has a plan and a purpose, is in control and desires the best for you?

## For reflection

### Scriptures

*'Our Father in heaven,*
*hallowed be your name,*
*your kingdom come,*
*your will be done …'*
(Matt. 6:9–10)

*'Teach me to do your will, for you are my God; may your good*
*Spirit lead me on level ground.'* (Psa. 143:10)

### Thought

As we submit our will to God each day, we need to ask Him to give us strength to live for Him and also to live for others.

### Action

Think back and make a note of any desires you had for your life that have not come to fruition. Can you see God's overall plan in the direction that He took you instead?

### Prayer

*I give you my regrets, problems, past, future, ambitions, dreams, weaknesses, habits and hurts. I give you my will and pray, Lord, may YOUR will be done in my life. Thank You that You are trustworthy at all times. Amen.*

## Chapter 4

# Commit your mind

*'Do not conform any longer to the pattern of this world,*
*but be transformed by the renewing of your mind.'*
Romans 12:2

J.B. Phillips' translation of Romans 12:2 says, 'Don't let the world around you squeeze you into its mould, but let God remould your minds from within …' Renewal of the mind involves God's divine work on our minds and also our proactive choices. C.S. Lewis once said, 'Where God is not, people see things in a completely different perspective.' Where God is not in our thinking, we end up with a distorted view of life. Every now and again my printer produces faint, blurry or distorted text and I have to realign and clean the print heads. In the same way our minds need to be realigned and cleansed. The longer we leave our minds unchallenged the more out of line our thinking becomes. The danger is that if left too long we get used to things being out of focus and this becomes our norm.

## How our minds work

What does your mind tend to be filled with? Is it positive or negative? Does it fit with the way you are described in Scripture as a child of God or does it contradict Scripture? What kind of thing do you tend to say to yourself that pull you down and affect the way you feel? What has happened in your past to influence the way you now think? Have you ever surrendered your mind to Christ and made a conscious decision to work on the various aspects of your mind?

I remember a young woman I counselled, Emma. She had been a Christian for ten years, had a strong faith and was actively involved in her church. She also had times when she suffered from depression and had mood swings. She easily felt threatened by others, was very jealous of them and was very competitive. Although she appeared to be very capable and confident she felt a failure and secretly turned to alcohol and food for comfort, which only compounded the feelings of self-loathing.

Dag Hammarskjöld said, 'A man who is at war with himself will be at war with others'[1] and that was so true of Emma. She had attempted to deal with the eating and drinking problems in various ways but nothing lasted, and she lived her life on the defensive. It was only when she had counselling that she realised her patterns of behaviour could not change until her mind changed. In the following months the work she carried out unfolded issues concerning insecurity, rejection and 'putdowns' as a child which resulted in the need to continually compete with others and be defensive in order to feel of value. Gradually, as her thought processes were addressed and she surrendered her mind, she began to see a change in her mood swings, her unhelpful reactions to other people and her tendency towards addictive patterns.

As Emma discovered, unless the mind is confronted and changed, other areas of our lives can remain enslaved. It is easy to assume that there is only really a need for a clean-up of our minds at conversion or if we are trapped in ungodly thought patterns, but most of us live with thought patterns and minds that have the tendency to weaken rather than strengthen our walk with God.

Our minds are closely connected to our thoughts and behaviour, and influence the way we relate to other people and to God. Proverbs notes the connection between thinking and behaviour: Proverbs 4:23 says, 'Be careful how you think; your life is shaped by your thoughts' (GNB). Proverbs 23:7 says, 'For as he thinks within himself, so he is' (NASB). How we think affects the way we feel, the choices we make and to what extent we pursue our relationship with God. The Hebrew word for 'thinks' in this passage is *shâ'ar* which, amongst other things, means to act as a gatekeeper. In biblical times the gate would lead into a walled city and the gatekeeper would guard who had access. As gatekeeper of your mind, what are you allowing in?

## Winning the battle

To act as a godly gatekeeper means becoming aware of the battles that take place in our mind. As I write this I am reminded of the book of Hosea. Hosea was a contemporary of Isaiah and Micah and the last prophet God called to challenge the people of Israel to repent. The picture portrayed in Hosea of God and Israel (and reflected in Hosea's own marriage) is of a loving husband yearning for a faithful wife but being faced with ongoing unfaithfulness.

Is it not similar in our lives? God yearns for us to recognise and respond to our need for a renewed mind, but we have the tendency to stray away from the truth and allow destructive thinking to take root. Hosea 4:6 says, 'My people are destroyed for lack of knowledge. ...' (NASB). Without the knowledge of what needs to change in our lives, and the ins and outs of the process of change, we can be defeated. Knowledge in this instance refers to insight, understanding, wisdom, discernment, etc. We require all these characteristics as we address the daily battles we encounter in our minds.

The mind is one area that Satan loves to attack and we tend to underestimate how destructive the enemy can be and how we can so easily be pulled into that destruction. In 2 Corinthians Paul says, 'We demolish arguments and every pretension that sets itself up against the knowledge of God, and we take captive every thought to make it obedient to Christ' (10:5). He understands fully the effect of a mind that is not captive to Christ and the extent to which there is a battle.

To win that battle we need to understand what is happening

in our minds. I couldn't explain it better than Neil Anderson and Dave Park who, in their book *Stomping out the Darkness* talk of the high-road and the low-road.

> We walk the high-road in our lives when we determine to learn God's plans for us in the Bible and commit ourselves to obey Him. We walk the low-road when we think thoughts and consider plans that are opposite of what God's Word says. We weaken our commitment to walking the high-road whenever we play around with ideas that are opposite to God's Word ...
>
> Where do low-road thoughts come from? There are two main sources.
>
> First our flesh still sparks low-road thoughts and ideas. The flesh is that part of us that was trained to live independently from God before we became Christians ... we didn't understand his ways and we learned to succeed and survive by our own abilities. Even though we now have a new nature in Christ the sinful world still tempts us to return to those old ways of thinking and living.
>
> Second, there is someone active in the world today who hates the high-road. Satan and his demons are busy trying to put negative, worldly patterns of thought into our minds which bring out negative, worldly patterns of behaviour.[2]

It is important to recognise the battle in our minds and to tackle it at a spiritual level without our focus being on the enemy. In 2 Corinthians Paul reminds us that 'The weapons we fight with are not the weapons of the world. On the contrary, they have divine power to demolish strongholds' (10:4). Strongholds are patterns of thought that have a *strong hold* over us and can become deeply ingrained in our minds through repetition over time or because of trauma. Common strongholds frequently include jealousy, anger, manipulation, hostility, addictions etc, the undermining of which involves taking thoughts captive, repentance, forgiveness and cutting ungodly ties to people, places and situations involved.

It is also important, as Paul tells us in his letter to the Ephesians, to 'Put on the full armour of God so that you can take your stand against the devil's schemes. For our struggle is not against flesh and blood, but against the rulers, against the authorities, against the powers of this dark world and against the spiritual forces of evil in the heavenly realms' (Eph. 6:11–12).

## The mind of Christ

We need to pray that we will think more like Jesus and become aware of the power of Christ to defeat the hold of the enemy. I have also found that an important part of my mind being renewed is asking God to bind my mind to His. In the Old Testament the Hebrew word *qasher* is used in conjunction with join together, knit, gird, bind. I like the concept of my mind being knit together with the mind of Christ.

Being knit together requires that our attitude is the same as that of Jesus (Phil. 2:5). Amongst other things, Jesus' attitude was one of humility. Augustine (AD 345–430) said, 'If you ask me what is the first precept of the Christian religion, I will answer, first, second and third, humility.' The philosopher John Ruskin (1819–1900) once said, 'I believe the first test of a truly great man is in his humility.'

While Selwyn Hughes highlights humility as one indicator of the Christian mind, his full list of a Christian mind is a mind 'that puts itself under the tutelage of Christ, is imbued with humility, is keenly perceptive, is accepting of authority, is disciplined in its thinking, is aware of the reality of good and evil, is undivided, and has an eternal perspective.'[3] I wonder how our minds compare with these descriptions? We can only really operate in this way if we surrender our mind to Christ on a daily basis and put our trust in God. If we put our trust in God then the peace of God will guard our hearts and minds (Phil. 4:7).

## For reflection

### Scriptures

*'Set your minds on things above, not on earthly things.'*
(Col. 3:2)

*'Test me, O LORD, and try me, examine my heart and my mind.'*
(Psa. 26:2)

### Thought

The more we surrender and are willing to submit to the teachings of Christ and the work of the Holy Spirit, the easier it becomes to fight thoughts that are not in line with Scripture.

### Action

Spend time today focusing on the cross and lay down wrong beliefs about yourself, others and God, allowing Him to renew your mind.

### Prayer

*Thank You, Lord, that I have the mind of Christ. Help me to surrender it to You every day so that you can develop it more in Your likeness. Amen.*

**Chapter 5**

# Offer your body

*'you were bought at a price.*
*Therefore honour God with your body.'*
1 Corinthians 6:20

In his epistle to the Romans Paul writes, 'Therefore, I urge you, brothers, in view of God's mercy, to offer your bodies as living sacrifices, holy and pleasing to God – this is your spiritual act of worship' (Rom. 12:1). When contemplating sacrifice and spiritual worship, the body is not always considered as relevant. The reason for this could be that the spiritual aspect of our lives is often perceived as something outside of the body, such as our *relationship* with God, our *prayer life*, our *use of the spiritual gifts* etc.

## A living sacrifice

Have you actually taken on board that you are called to offer your *body* as a living sacrifice and that your *body* is to be *holy* and *pleasing* to God? What is your attitude towards your body? When we understand that it is our bodies themselves that are the place where the Holy Spirit lives, we see all the more how important it is to surrender them and to keep them clean before the Lord so that they can be vessels for Him to use.

We live in an age and culture where the body is idolised and where there is constant pressure to perfect the body and reverse the aging process, often in ways unattainable by the majority. If you asked those in the model industry what was meant by a *pleasing* body, they would probably emphasise the importance of leanness, body proportion, height and aesthetic beauty. In fact for some this has been taken to such extremes that what is promoted and idolised is outside of that which in medical terms is deemed healthy.

Focusing on body image and worshipping the body is not what Paul means through his use of 'holy and pleasing'. Holy and pleasing has more to do with the fact that:

... our bodies must not be made the instruments of sin and uncleanness, but set apart for God, and put to holy uses. It is the soul that is the proper subject of holiness; but a sanctified soul communicates a holiness to the body ... when the bodily actions are so, the body is holy.[1]

Pleasing in the world's terms for many can end up being a form of entrapment; pleasing in spiritual terms is a part of our freedom because it results in our reflecting the image of Christ. We are to care for our bodies, but not worship them, and we are to aspire to holiness of conduct, not perfection of the material.

What counts to God is so different from what counts to the world. We need to hold on to the words God spoke to Samuel when he was mourning Saul (whom God had removed as king) and wondering who would become the anointed one: 'The LORD does not look at the things man looks at. Man looks at the outward appearance, but the LORD looks at the heart' (1 Sam. 16:7).

As well as assessing my attitude of heart I have come to learn that for my body to be holy and pleasing to the Lord I need to evaluate my health, eating habits, exercise levels, sleep patterns and stress levels on a regular basis. We have a responsibility for what we put into our bodies and how we treat them. If our bodies are to be used by God, we need to take care of them as we would take care of Jesus if He Himself were with us in body.

## Caring for the temple

The reason it is so important to look after our bodies is highlighted in Paul's letter to the Corinthians: 'Don't you know that you yourselves are God's temple and that God's Spirit lives in you?' (1 Cor. 3:16). 'For we are the temple of the living God' (2 Cor. 6:16). In the Old Testament, and in Jesus' time, the Temple was the place of sacrifice, but in AD 70 Titus (a future Roman emperor and son of Vespasian, the Roman emperor at the time) destroyed the Temple and the place of sacrifice was taken away.

Those of us who have given our lives to Jesus know that through His death and resurrection He became a substitute for the Temple (John 2:19–21), providing the way for us to be reconciled once and for all to the Father. In view of this, we now have the privilege of offering our bodies as living sacrifices. But I wonder if we really do count it a privilege? Do we have the same regard for our bodies, the temple of the Holy Spirit, as the Jews did, long ago, of Solomon's and then Herod's Temple?

At the times when we are most challenged about caring for the temple of the Holy Spirit and surrendering our bodies, it is good to remind ourselves that Jesus first surrendered Himself for us: His body, soul and spirit were offered in exchange for our salvation. I came across a beautiful prayer by Jan Sutch Pickard, a part of which I would like to share with you as a reminder of what Jesus endured for us.

## Prayer of the Crucified

Look at these feet:
they walked the dusty roads
they walked into so many homes
of neighbours, strangers, lonely people.
These feet danced at weddings
and went to the graveyard
to bring back Lazarus.

They were soothed with ointment
by a woman no one else wanted to touch.
And now they are nailed to the cross
with iron nails forced through skin, sinew and bone
into splintering wood.
These feet cannot walk in your world anymore.
My God, why? ...

Look at these hands:
they made tables, tools, toys
in the carpenter's workshop;
they reached out in love
to people who were in pain, outsiders,
and healed and helped them;
they plucked ears of corn,
they drew patterns in the sand;
they washed tired feet,
they broke bread to share among friends.
And now they are broken,
they are caked with dirt and blood,
they are pierced through the palm
with cruel nails.
These fingers curl and stretch in agony.
There is nothing else they can do.
My God, why? ...

Look at this head:
It used to turn to the single voice in the crowd,
the outsider.
It bent
to be alongside and listen to children.
It fell asleep on a pillow

in the bows of a boat in a big storm,
trusting in God.
Long ago it fell asleep
on a mother's breast.
Now it is restless
on the rough wood of the cross
with an unbelieving slogan pinned above,
with a mocking crown of thorns
pressed down on the tender skin
of the forehead,
so that blood
runs into the eyes, already blinded
with tears of pain.
My God, why?[2]

## Communicating God's heart

Because of Jesus' surrendered body we can now offer our bodies and allow them to be used by Him on earth. How we conduct our lives, what we do practically and how we come across should speak of Jesus.

Only yesterday, in church, a lady stood up and gave her testimony: an important part of her journey to salvation was Christians exampling Jesus. She had been brought up as an atheist and had a stereotypical view of Christians. Then she was assigned a boss at work, a Christian who demonstrated the non-judgmental, unconditional regard of Jesus. A stranger, who also happened to be a Christian, started cutting her grass, expecting nothing in return. A neighbour, again a Christian, answered the questions that were emerging in her about God and led her to the books in the Bible that were most easily understood by a non-believer.

These people used their bodies and their conduct to demonstrate Jesus to a woman who for years had adamantly denied the existence of God. Consequently she gave her life to Him and is now in the position of offering the same example of Jesus to others.

The testimony of which I have just spoken shows that our hands, along with other parts of our body, play an important part in communicating God's heart. With what do your hands tend to be filled – work, baggage, burdens and 'must dos'? How powerful our hands would be if they were surrendered to God at all times. Each moment of the day we are being led to use our hands by God, but do we realise? We may be led to write a letter, make a phone call, reach out with compassion, help lift another's burdens, turn the pages of God's Word. The Holy Spirit lives in us and, as we reach out and touch the life of another, we are actually taking Jesus to that person, be it in comfort, reassurance, encouragement or practical help.

Surrendering our hands is about offering them to God for His service; allowing Him to dwell within us and direct us. Do you ask God to guide your hands? Have you ever anointed your hands or had them anointed? Do you pray for your hands or allow others to pray for them?

As a Christian writer I pray for my hands together with what I write and, at times, have been led powerfully by God. However, recently I was listening to a talk on the life of Frances Ridley Havergal and I was struck by her admission that she didn't write a single word until the Lord directed her. When she was writing the hymn 'Take My Life', she began by praying, 'Lord, what do you want me to write for the first line?' When He told her she would move onto the next, 'Lord, what do you want me to write for the second line?' In guiding her to write that hymn we see not only the extent of her own surrender but the extent to which God longs for us to surrender, lovingly and wholeheartedly, each area of our lives to Him.

## All of who we are

God can use any part of us to impact the life of another: our words, smile, eyes and ability to listen. However, we need to be mindful of how we come across because, it is said that 55 per cent of communication is through non-verbal behaviour (facial expression, arm and body movement and body posture), 38 per cent through tone of voice (inflection, how things are said) and *only* 7 per cent through actual spoken words. This means that whilst our intentions to be channels for God to use are good our human failings frequently let us down, and hence it is important to be willing to allow God to knock off our rough edges and to submit our weaknesses to Him. Our most deeply ingrained weaknesses can become our strengths if we allow God to turn them around. When we surrender our bodies we are, in effect, saying to God, 'Use me in the way that You see best.' May He do just that.

## For reflection

### Scriptures
*'Do you not know that your bodies are members of Christ himself?'* (1 Cor. 6:15)

*'Now you are the body of Christ, and each one of you is a part of it.'* (1 Cor. 12:27)

### Thought
Our attitude towards our bodies needs to reflect God's attitude towards us.

### Action
Consider the ways in which you could make yourself available to God and be used by Him. Think too of both your attitude towards, and regard for, your body. Do you need to make any changes?

### Prayer
*Lord, I surrender my body afresh to You and I ask that You will show me ways in which I can be more mindful of my body in order that it will honour You. Amen.*

## Chapter 6

# Hand over your time

*'Be very careful, then, how you live – not as unwise but as wise, making the most of every opportunity ...'*
Ephesians 5:15

I n any one day we all have twenty-four hours, which is equivalent to 1,440 minutes or 86,400 seconds. I wonder how we use these moments and if in God's economy it is the best use of our time? One day can so easily blur into another: days, weeks, months and years have the tendency to pass by at an alarming rate.

As a self-motivated person I often find that I live with a sense of being driven and time running out. However, the more I have explored the path of surrender and its connection to freedom, the more I have come to realise that letting go of my own agenda and handing time over to God is significant. I have come to witness that surrendering time often leads to a cleaning-up process as God reorders and prioritises our time, our moments. It is similar to the cleaning-up process on a computer when the operator goes into 'Performance and Maintenance' and rearranges items on the hard disk to enable programmes to run more efficiently. Effectively files are reordered and condensed, eradicating wasted space. How we need that in our lives.

## Making every minute count

Psalm 118 reminds us that today (and every day) is the day that God has made (v.24). Is God in charge of your day? How much do you plan your days and your moments, and how much do you leave your moments and your day open to God's leading? Are you happy to see your plans change? I work a lot to deadlines and so a fairly high degree of structure is necessary. I have tended to be the kind of person that likes to plan my time to the minute and in the past used to become quite stressed if anything unplanned ate into my 'work slot'. I might have changed what I was doing but inside I could hear myself calculating how many hours I'd have to add on to the day to make up for 'wasted time'.

Recently God has been bringing about a significant change: as I commit my moments to Him I find that my work is taking less time and if other things, led by Him, do come along and take the 'designated work slot' then amazingly the inspiration needed for my work flows at twice the pace. He is in the process of teaching me that if I can trust Him with my moments then He will give back to me more than I have given up.

As we do what *God* wants us to do, rather than what *we* want or 'ought' to do, it seems that He redeems time. The key here is doing what *God* wants us to do; we cannot expect Him to redeem time when we operate outside of His will. Twice in the Old Testament God altered time significantly. In Joshua 10 God caused time to stop for several hours in order that Israel could achieve victory (vv.12–14). In Isaiah 38 there is the account of the turning back of the sundial ten degrees for Hezekiah's benefit (vv.7–8). This dramatic change to time may not have occurred since but somehow God does seem to enable us to accomplish things that He ordains more than time would normally permit, hence 'stretching time'.

We are all answerable to God for how we use our time. It is good to remind ourselves, as Mart De Haan writes: 'Significance is not found in the number of our days, but in what our eternal God says about how we have used them.'[1] Solomon tells us that we '… must give an account … for everything [we] do' (Eccl. 11:9, NLT). Moses, in Psalm 90 prays, 'Teach us to use wisely all the time we have' (v.12, CEV). The NLT puts it this way, 'Teach us to realize the brevity of life, so that we may grow in wisdom.' I have come to see that making the most of our time is about allowing the moments to matter and ensuring that they are handed over to God. If I have chosen to give my life, my self and my moments to God then in fact my time also belongs to Him.

By surrendering our time we are, effectively, asking God to lead us and guide us in what our time consists of. Paul, in his letter to the Ephesians, writes: '… make every minute count' (5:16, CEV). Do we? To fulfil these words we need to examine how we use our time and whether what we do is: a) what God is calling us to do; b) what others are dictating; c) what we are inwardly being driven to do; d) what we take on to please others rather than please God.

## A time for everything

Ecclesiastes 3 reveals that God sovereignly predetermines all of life's activities in stating that there is a time for everything: 'a time to be born and a time to die, a time to plant and a time to uproot' (v.2) Soon after I became a Christian and read Ecclesiastes I questioned if there was any point in surrendering my moments if God has it all worked out anyway! But now I tend to look at it differently – God has a plan for my life but holding on to my moments adds unnecessary complexities. It reminds me of the Israelites taking forty years to enter the promised land when in fact it was only a stone's throw away.

I wonder what the moments for each and every Israelite were made up of over that forty-year period? Were they wasted? Were they productive? Were they given over to God? I wonder too how different *our* days would be if our moments were always surrendered and *really were* kept for Jesus! Anne Morrow Lindbergh, an American writer, once said, 'If you surrender completely to the moments as they pass, you live more richly those moments.'[2] How true. Do you sometimes think, 'I'd like to live more richly'? Do you feel that life is futile and there is more to life than the years just passing by? Surrendering our moments brings with it a whole new way of living and a completely different way of looking at life. Could it be that surrendering our moments and trusting God with them is actually a part of what we often call 'living by faith'?

Jesus conducted His life very much along the principle of time surrendered to His Father. In response to being 'picked up' by the Pharisees for working on the Sabbath, 'Jesus gave them this answer: "I tell you the truth, the Son can do nothing by himself; he can do only what he sees his Father doing, because whatever the Father does the Son also does"' (John 5:19). Jesus did that which was not expected of Him (heal on the Sabbath) and He didn't do that which was expected of Him (heal everyone or respond to their needs immediately). Jesus knew that the answer lay in listening to His Father, not in cramming more into the time He had. His moments were totally surrendered to His Father and not one was wasted.

## Into God's hands

Surrendering our moments requires us to put the direction, the content and timing of our day into God's hands. This doesn't mean to say that having a schedule is wrong and we have to be highly spontaneous, but that we are open to God working in our lives (be it with or without a given schedule). The basic assumption of surrendering aspects of our lives to God is that He will use them to His glory. So, when we surrender our time we are trusting that God will use our time for His purposes.

This month I had a clear example of surrendered moments and the fruit such surrender brings. I was waiting at the bus stop to go into town when I noticed a British Telecom van drive up the lane. My telephone line wasn't working and I urgently needed to find out what was happening. Instinct said 'Forget the bus and chase BT', but having made a conscious effort that morning to surrender my day and my moments to the Lord, I knew God was prompting me to catch the bus.

Part way through the bus journey I saw someone stand up and squeeze past the person next to her, saying, 'Excuse me, I want to speak to that lady over there.' To my surprise I realised that the woman, probably in her early seventies, was making a beeline for the seat next to me! What on earth did she want to talk to me about? She sat down and promptly asked if she could have a look at what I was reading. I had in my hand a very old copy of *Every Day with Jesus*.

'I thought so,' she smiled. 'Are you a born-again Christian?'

'I certainly am,' I replied.

What followed was an account of how she had not long moved to rural Gower and was cut off from her supply of reading material and Christian fellowship. She had read *Every Day with Jesus* years ago and didn't know how to get hold of it now. I promptly tore out the back page and handed her an order form. I then gave her the name and address of Nicholaston House, the Christian Retreat Centre on Gower where I work (which 'just happens' to be only a short way from where she lives) and invited her to our next event. Her face lit up.

My surrendered moments turned into meaningful moments for both the stranger on the bus and for me; and maybe our conversation impacted the people sitting behind too!

## Appreciating our moments

Our moments are our time, and time is a precious commodity in our increasingly busy and hectic world. My logic told me I needed to use my time to go back up the lane and speak to the

BT man, but my spirit was aware of something more important. Surrendering our moments means 'tuning in' and hearing God as well as actually handing time itself over to Him.

When we do this, we are assured that He keeps our moments secure and uses them for good. Our moments are a lot safer in God's hands than in ours. Not only do we have a tendency to mess things up but what is in our hands is at more risk of being destroyed by the enemy. However, we need to make sure that we not only *give* or *offer* our moments to God but that we actually *entrust* them into His care. Often we attempt to give over our moments and yet at the same time still stay in control. In reality we cannot do both successfully: either we *give* our moments or we *keep* them. Which are you going to choose today?

# For reflection

### Scriptures
*'For there is a proper time and procedure for every matter ...'*
(Eccl. 8:6)

*'Sow for yourselves righteousness, reap the fruit of unfailing love, and break up your unploughed ground; for it is time to seek the LORD, until he comes and showers righteousness on you.'*
(Hosea 10:12)

### Thought
Un-surrendered moments can too easily lead to 'if only' and regret. Surrendered moments can be transformed moments. If in the next twenty-four hours you were conscious of God standing next to you every minute of the day, how would you use the time differently?

### Action
Spend a little time at the start of each day considering how you can make best use of your time. Offer the day to God and ask Him to take your moments and use them.

### Prayer
*Lord, help me each day to give You my hours and my moments and not simply to fill them with my own agenda. Amen.*

**Chapter 7**

# Choose your words

'Let your conversation be always full of grace, seasoned with salt,
so that you may know how to answer everyone.'
Colossians 4:6

**M**atthew, in his Gospel, reminds us that '… out of the overflow of the heart the mouth speaks' (12:34). In Psalm 12, David tells God of his despair over the way people talk: 'They speak falsehood to one another; With flattering lips and with a double heart they speak' (v.2, NASB). In Psalm 141 David also asks God to: 'Set a guard over my mouth, O LORD; keep watch over the door of my lips' (v.3). The root word referred to in the Old Testament for *lips* includes speech, language, thoughts and motivation. Scripture encourages us to guard our lips and tells us that 'He who guards his lips guards his life …' (Prov. 13:3). Guarding our lips means watching our words.

I came across a little anonymous poem which is a light-hearted reminder for us to be mindful of what we say:

If your lips would keep from slips
Five things observe with care:
Of whom you speak, to whom you speak,
And how and when and where.

## Godless chatter

As the poem indicates, we must be careful concerning of whom we speak and how. Scripture also warns us to be mindful of the manner and content of our speech. 'Do not let any unwholesome talk come out of your mouths, but only what is helpful for building others up according to their needs, that it may benefit those who listen' (Eph. 4:29). It is not only overtly unwholesome talk that we are told to avoid but 'worldly *and* empty chatter, for it will lead to further ungodliness' (2 Tim. 2:16, NASB, italics mine). *Worldly* refers to that which lacks relationship of affinity to God; *empty* refers to chatter that is devoid of moulding our lives as believers. I wonder how much of our talk fits these descriptions, or has the tendency to come precariously close?

The consequence of ungodly talk is that, as Paul warns Timothy, and hence us, it will 'spread like gangrene' (2 Tim. 2:17). The New Testament Greek for such ungodliness, *asebela*, speaks of a lack of reverence and a neglect of duty towards God, our neighbour and ourselves. Perhaps most of us would rightly say that our talk is not lacking in reverence, but we would have to admit that there is, at times, a neglect of duty towards God, our neighbour and ourselves.

## Power of life and death

Many of us tend to underestimate the power of our words, their effect upon others and the right we give to the enemy to cause disruption in our lives through what we say and the attitudes we hold. The power of words is one of the major themes of the book of Proverbs, a book of wisdom. In fact the mouth, lips, tongue and words are referred to more than 150 times in Proverbs. Take a look at just a few of the references:

- 'A fool's lips bring him strife …' (Prov.18:6)
- 'A fool's mouth is his undoing, and his lips are a snare to his soul.' (Prov. 18:7)
- 'Truthful lips endure for ever, but a lying tongue lasts only a moment.' (Prov. 12:19)
- 'Reckless words pierce like a sword, but the tongue of the wise brings healing.' (Prov. 12:18)
- 'The right word at the right time is like precious gold set in silver.' (Prov. 25:11, CEV)
- 'He who guards his mouth and his tongue keeps himself

from calamity.' (Prov. 21:23)

- 'Pleasant words are a honeycomb, sweet to the soul and healing to the bones.' (Prov. 16:24)
- 'The tongue that brings healing is a tree of life ...' (Prov. 15:4)
- 'A perverse man stirs up dissension, and a gossip separates close friends.' (Prov. 16:28)
- 'A gossip betrays a confidence; so avoid a man who talks too much.' (Prov. 20:19)

Proverbs doesn't beat around the bush when it tells us that 'The tongue has the power of life and death ...' (18:21). Life signifies living purposefully whereas death signifies destruction. Do the words you speak about others result in purposefulness or destruction for the other person? What about the words you speak about yourself? We would do well to consider carefully the words we speak because, as Selwyn Hughes once said, 'Every word you utter becomes flesh – in you.'

Words either build us up or tear us down and they have the power to enrich or erode the life of another. I am currently researching a book on bullying and I am finding that negative words play a significant part in the scars left by bullying. From what people are sharing, and from my own experience of being bullied, the unkind words of others have as much power to control the life of an individual for years to come as acts of physical cruelty do.

In his epistle, James warns us that the tongue has the tendency to be restless and full of poison and needs taming. He points out that 'Out of the same mouth come praise and cursing' and '... this should not be' (3:10). Most of us are not in a position of bullying and tearing the life of another apart, but our tongues are at risk of speaking less than positively about others, both directly and behind their backs.

We need wisdom when we speak. James goes on to teach us about two kinds of wisdom – worldly and godly. We must seek godly wisdom. '… wisdom that comes from heaven is first of all pure; then peace-loving, considerate, submissive, full of mercy and good fruit, impartial and sincere' (3:17). The answer as to how we attain such wisdom appears in James 4, 'Submit yourselves, then, to God …' (v.7)

If we are to live godly lives, as well as submitting ourselves to God we need to surrender our words: surrendering our words includes surrender of our tone of voice and the body language that accompanies what we say. In the same way, we must surrender our thoughts; after all, thoughts are merely words spoken internally. Paul commends us to think on whatever is true, noble, right, pure, lovely, admirable, excellent and praiseworthy (Phil. 4:8). It's good to remember the following: that which our lips, mouths and words utter, our lives must reflect and not contradict.

## Wisdom with words

Whilst the words we say internally to ourselves may be destructive, we can at least learn to correct what we say and undo some of the damage. However, what we say to others and others say to us is less easily undone. Once words are out they can't be hauled back in again, as Ray Prichard illustrates in his book *The ABC's of Wisdom*:

> Once upon a time a man said something about his neighbour that was untrue. The word spread around the village as one person told another. But soon the truth came out – what could the man do? He went to see the village priest, and the priest gave him some strange instructions.

'Take a bag full of feathers and place one feather on the doorstep of each person who heard the untrue story you told. Then go back a day later, pick up the feathers, and bring the bag back to me.'

So the man did as the priest said. But when he went back to pick up the feathers, nearly all of them were gone. When he went back to the priest, he said, 'Father, I did as you said but when I went back the wind had blown the feathers away and I could not get them back.' And the priest replied, 'So it is with careless words, my son. Once they are spoken, they cannot be taken back. You may ask forgiveness for what you said, but you cannot take your words back ...'[1]

Are there words that you have spoken which you now regret and of which you would like to repent – perhaps gossip, put-downs, words said in haste? Ray Prichard offers the following suggestion concerning things we say about other people:[2]

If you must share what you know, use three questions as guides before telling what you know to someone else.

Is it true?

Is it kind?

Is it necessary?

There wouldn't be any gossip if we used these three questions before speaking.

Frances Ridley Havergal, in her book, *Kept for the Master's Use*, shares a beautiful prayer she once heard which affirms what I have been saying:

Lord, take my lips,
and speak through them;
take my mind,

and think through it;
take my heart,
and set it on fire.

Let's pray that prayer for ourselves, from our hearts, and follow it with the words of the psalmist: 'May my lips overflow with praise, for you teach me your decrees. May my tongue sing of your word, for all your commands are righteous' (Psa. 119:171–172).

## For reflection

### Scriptures
*'May the words of my mouth and the meditation of my heart be pleasing in your sight, O LORD, my Rock and my Redeemer.'*
(Psa. 19:14)

*'The mouth of the righteous is the fountain of life ...'* (Prov. 10:11)

### Thought
Words have the power to shape and mould the life of an individual. What words from the past drive and control you? How do these affect your relationships with others?

### Action
What unhelpful words do you tend to say about yourself or others? Can you replace these with words of encouragement?

### Prayer
*Father, I ask for Your forgiveness for the words that I have spoken which have crushed or discouraged me or others in any way. Amen.*

**Chapter 8**

# Expand your love

*'And this is my prayer: that your love may abound more and more …'*
Philippians 1:9

Surrendering our love and making a choice to expand our love are essential aspects of our maturity as believers because '…while knowledge may make a man look big, it is only love that can make him grow to his full stature' (1 Cor. 8:1, Phillips). Sophocles (496–406 BC) once said, 'One word frees us of all the pain and weight of life. That one word is love'. The reason that love frees us is because God is love (1 John 4:16) and when we operate in love, His life is breathed into us and is operating through us.

Dr W.E. Sangster, a famous Methodist preacher, made it clear that 'those who manifest God's love are those who have had a blinding realisation of the love of God and whose own love flames in response'. We can't try to love; we must let God fan the flame of love as we bask in His love. My friend, Sue (mentioned in the Introduction) began to cry out to God one day because she found it hard to love other people. She went through a period of suffering and refining after which it seems God gave her a new heart filled with His Spirit and His love. She describes it as 'a love that seems to increase the more I give love out'. She now finds that however many people God brings along her path, there is the capacity to love them because, as she explains, 'It's not my love, but God's love in me.'

## Radiating love

The love of Christ is a radiating love – it is a love that flows out to others, not a love that feeds self. Our un-surrendered love has the tendency to consume or want something in return. It can be manipulative, self-gratifying and full of wrong motives. It can also have pay-offs, lead to burn out and result in an unhealthy desire for material things, success and unrealistic expectations of people. In contrast, as David Roper once pointed out, 'Jesus teaches us to measure our lives by losses rather than gains, by sacrifices rather than self-preservation, by time spent for others rather than time lavished upon ourselves, by love poured out rather than love poured in.'[1]

Selwyn Hughes offers the following advice concerning our desire to love more: 'Don't try to manufacture love. Linger in the shadow of the cross. The love of God finds its most burning expression there.'[2] Frances Ridley Havergal put it this way: 'Only love understands love.' So, if we want to expand our love we must spend time receiving God's love.

Scripture gives various accounts and pictures of God's love and makes it clear that He loves us despite our unworthiness. Hosea 3 speaks of the woman beloved and yet adulterous. Are we too not like that at times – overwhelmingly loved by God despite our unfaithfulness? His love still flows out to us in abundance even though we look away from Him with eyes that wander towards the world, seek earthly pleasure and self-gratification. His love even continues to pour over us, although it grieves Him when we put our trust in people rather than Him and indulge in false or futile comfort and hope.

Another powerful image of God's tender, life-giving love is found in the Song of Moses (Deut. 32). The theme of the song is the name of the Lord, His loving care of His people, His righteousness and His mercy, which is contrasted with the unfaithfulness of Israel. In verse 10 the passage speaks of God's love for Israel as the 'apple of his eye', which some versions translate as the 'pupil of his eye'. The pupil is the part of the eye upon which sight so greatly depends; it is a very delicate part which needs protection no matter what. Do you know that as God's child you too are the apple of God's eye and that He protects you at great cost?

In verse 11 of Deuteronomy 32, reference is made to the eagle. The eagle recognises when her young are ready and kicks them out of the nest. But she flies close by ready to swoop under those that do not fly but fall and she carefully catches them in her vast expanse of wing. The mother eagle has huge regard for her young and in teaching them to fly she protects and encourages them to imitate her own movements. In the same way God loves us so much that whilst He kicks us out of the nest (encourages our growth), He watches out for us and is ready to catch us. He also longs that we would imitate His ways; imitate His love.

Amongst other things, through His love God offers us:

- **Comfort** (Psa. 119:76) – God calls us to His side. He exhorts and consoles us. He soothes us in times of grief and fear.

- **Support** (Psa. 94:18) – He lends strength to us, holds us in position and prevents us from falling, sinking or slipping.

- **Guidance** (Psa. 25:5) – He leads and directs in the way we should go.

- **Affirmation** (Zeph. 3:17) – God's love expresses His delight in us and affirmation of us.

- **Protection** (Psa. 32:7) – He is our hiding place. He protects us from trouble and surrounds us with songs of deliverance. The word surround comes from the same verb as 'encompass'. We are encompassed or encircled by God's love and deliverance, and there is no safer place to be.

## Out of the overflow

We are dearly loved by God; so greatly loved, in fact, that it was out of the overflow of His love that we even came into being. Cardinal Hume once summed up this thought by saying, 'We love people because they are there, but with God it is the other way round: because he loves them they are there.'

'… He [God] picked us out for Himself as His own – in Christ before the foundation of the world; that we should be holy and blameless in His sight … He foreordained us to be adopted as His own children through Jesus Christ, in accordance with the purpose of His will – because it pleased Him …' (Eph. 1:4–5, Amp). What incredible love the Father has for us, and when we realise the extent of that love, our hearts seek after Him. 'Then you will seek Me, inquire for *and* require Me (as a vital necessity) and find Me; when you search for Me with all your heart, I will be found by you, says the Lord, and I will release you from captivity …' (Jer. 29:13–14, Amp).

Loving God more and more helps us to keep our love of others and material possessions in perspective. If we do not seek after God with all our heart and, in so doing, discover the depth of His love for us it can be easy to deviate into seeking happiness in the form of conditional love. It's not that we love others too much, but that we love God too little. Without the certainty of God's unconditional love for us and our expression of love for Him we can end up manoeuvring our world in order to feel safe, and so fail to relate to God and others in a way that brings satisfaction.

When we seek after God with all our heart and spend time in His presence, His love flows in abundance, and we are more able to love both others and ourselves. God's love and acceptance of us as we are, despite our failings, lays the foundation for us to love and accept ourselves, which in turn is the prerequisite to loving others, because as John Powell points out, 'If I do not love myself, I can only *use* others; I cannot *love* them'.[3]

If we remain in God and our love flows out of His fountain of love, we are able to draw close to others, and as we put on the breastplate of love (1 Thess. 5:8), it makes it safe for us to do so. We do not have to fear that we will be hurt or rejected by them, for there 'is no fear in love' (1 John 4:18). To be rid of that fear we must put our dependency not in the unstable reactions of other people but in God, our solid rock, until in boldness we can say, 'I depend on God alone; I put my hope in him. He alone protects and saves me; he is my defender, and I shall never be defeated' (Psa. 62:5–6, GNB).

## Not in isolation

The key to fruitful love is the *source* of love. If we draw upon that which is of our own making more effort is needed and there is a limited supply of love. But if we draw upon that which God gives us, the more we give the more we have. Frances Ridley Havergal once put it this way: 'We have a sealed treasure of love, which either remains sealed, and then gradually dries up and wastes away, or is unsealed and poured out, and yet is the fuller and not the emptier for the outpouring.'

In his second letter to the Corinthians, Paul tells us that 'Christ's love compels us' (5:14). Something that compels is rousing, strong, and brings about interest, conviction, attention and admiration. There is nothing weak or ineffective about the love of Christ. In the same way, our receiving His love to pass on is not without positive consequence. As we love others with the love which Jesus has given us, we draw them closer to His love. We do not love that they may love us, but that they may love Him.

The evidence that the love we pour out is from Jesus and not of our own making is that it doesn't occur in isolation. Love is, after all, just one part of the fruit of the Spirit: 'But the fruit of the Spirit is love, joy, peace, patience, kindness, goodness, faithfulness, gentleness and self-control' (Gal. 5:22–23).

## Love is …

I remember as a child being fascinated by the 'Love is …' sayings. But all the 'love is …' sayings and our own examples of love are nothing compared to Paul's words about love in 1 Corinthians 13. A friend of mine, Jackie, wrote a beautiful meditation on Paul's words. I suggest you take time to reflect on the words and allow them to sink in and consider how your love matches the descriptions.

- **Love is patient.** Patience is waiting, patience will wait, patience is until 'it' happens, whatever 'it' is. Patience is about tolerating each other's mistakes and stupidities. It is forbearance, serenity, long-suffering and perseverance.

- **Love is kind.** Kindness is about having a heart of compassion, particularly for the unlovely. It's about giving a hand or a hug when you least feel like it. It is about being considerate, generous, thoughtful and understanding. You can't be kind with a hard heart; therefore it is being tender-hearted. You cannot be kind and avoid your neighbour; kindness is about being neighbourly.

- **Love does not envy.** Envy is your pain and discontentment about another's success or superiority. Envy compares you with others with dissatisfaction; it doesn't recognise that you are a limited edition of one. Envy covets another's looks, relationships, status, possessions and even their spirituality. Envy is never content.

- **Love does not boast.** It does not say or think, 'I am better than you', 'I am more spiritual than you', 'I feel superior to you'.

- **Love is not proud.** Pride easily gets offended, is often oversensitive. Pride says, 'How dare they!', 'How could you!', 'Why me?' Pride only breeds quarrels and discontent.

- **Love is not rude.** It does not abuse, is not abrupt, and is always respectful, even when wronged.

- **Love is not self-seeking.** It never says, 'Me first', it always thinks more highly of others than oneself.

- **Love is not easily angered.** It always tries to see things from the other's point of view. It always listens well before responding. It doesn't jump to conclusions but is self-controlled and calm.

- **Love keeps no record of wrongs.** It is unconditional. It does not harbour resentments to throw up when convenient. It does not become bitter but always forgives.

- **Love does not delight in evil but rejoices with the truth.** It hates sin but celebrates honesty. It speaks the truth, risking rejection and receives the truth even when it hurts.

- **Love always protects.** It never exposes or humiliates.

- **Love always trusts.** It always gives another chance.

- **Love always hopes.** It always looks for the good and believes for the good.

- **Love always perseveres.** It does things time and time again and never gives up.

- **Love never fails.**

Jesus perfectly embodies God's love. The Greek word for such love is *agape*; a self-sacrificial love that seeks the good of all (Rom. 15:2) and manifests itself in servanthood. Jesus did nothing out of selfish ambition or vain conceit, but out of humility (Phil. 2:3) took on the very nature of a servant (Phil. 2:7). Through this act, it is clear that servanthood and unconditional love are synonymous. It is also clear that Jesus entrusted Himself to God (1 Pet. 2:23), because He was secure in God's love for Him.

When we, fallible human beings, use the word love it tends to be more of a *phileō* love, which means to be a friend, or an *eros* love, which is romantic. Both of these are focused on feelings, unlike *agape*, which is not feelings-based but is a sacrificial love that chooses to love. Jesus didn't *feel* like going to the cross. He made a *choice* to go to the cross; it was a decision based on an act of love. God doesn't love us because He *feels* like loving us but because He is holy and morally perfect, and His nature is love. As Thomas à Kempis (1380–1471) once said, 'Love feels no burden, thinks nothing of trouble, attempts what is above its strength, pleads no excuse of impossibility; for it thinks all things lawful for itself, and all things possible.' If we could love according to Thomas à Kempis's definition and with the *agape* love of Jesus, what a difference we would make in our lives and the lives of others.

## For reflection

### Scriptures

*'And this is my prayer: that your love may abound more and more …'* (Phil. 1:9)

*'Dear children, let us not love with words or tongue but with actions and in truth.'* (1 John 3:18)

### Thought

Love is the pivot from which all in our life must be directed: 'Love rules the court, the camp, the grove and men below and heaven above; for love is heaven and heaven is love' (Sir Walter Scott).

### Action

Think about the ways in which God's love has changed you. Does your love for others release change in them?

### Prayer

*Thank You that You have created me to love but help me to draw on Your resources and not simply my own. Open my eyes to the times when I have not acted in love. Teach me what it is to love sacrificially; not only to love when I want to but when it actually costs me to do so. Amen.*

## Chapter 9

# Live out your worship

*'ascribe to the LORD the glory due to his name.*
*Bring an offering and come before him; worship*
*the LORD in the splendour of his holiness.'*
1 Chronicles 16:29

To live out our worship is to give God all aspects of our self in worship (heart, will, mind, body, time, words, love). Rick Warren says, 'The heart of worship is surrender',[1] and Isaac Watts (1674–1748) in his famous hymn, 'When I Survey the Wondrous Cross', makes the same point through his words, 'love so amazing, so divine, demands my soul, my life, my all!' The fact is that God deserves more than simply our words in worship. If we can give Him our soul, our life, our all, then I believe our worship will be taken into a new dimension; as will our praise, since praise and worship are so closely linked.

King David was a man who realised the connection between the giving of himself in surrender and the increase that this brought about in his praise and worship of God. We saw in Chapter 2 how David's surrendered heart resulted in a significant change in him and set him apart from others. By his writings throughout the Psalms and what he declares in 2 Samuel 23, it would appear that it had an impact on his worship too, as he declares, 'The Spirit of the LORD spoke through me; his word was on my tongue' (2 Sam. 23:2). Rather than singing songs that other people had written, David worships through his own songs, proclaiming God as his rock, his fortress, his deliverer, his shield, the horn of his salvation, his stronghold, his refuge and his saviour (2 Sam. 22:2–3).

David worshipped God both for who He is and what He does. He knew the reality of finding freedom as he worshipped, and worshipping because God had granted him freedom. He would no doubt have agreed with the words in *Our Daily Bread*, 'Praise is the song of a soul set free.'[2]

## Worship is key!

Worship was integral to David's walk with the Lord. Is it integral to yours? How much do you worship God? Besides worshipping Him with others, do you worship Him on your own? We see how vital worship is simply by observing the number of times it is mentioned in the Bible. There are some 560 worship-related scriptures. In addition, the biggest book in the Bible, the Psalms, is a book which focuses largely on worship.

The account of the Magi visiting the young Jesus also shows clearly the priority of worship. We tend to see the Magi as rich men bearing gifts of great worth, but in fact the first thing they chose to do was worship the King of kings. 'On coming to the house, they saw the child with his mother Mary, and they bowed down and worshipped him' (Matt. 2:11). If it had been you or me coming to see Jesus, we would probably have handed over our precious gifts before anything else! The New American Standard Bible expresses that the Magi *fell down* and worshipped; in order to fall down they would have had to lay aside their gifts. Their worship of Jesus came before all else.

## Develop the lifestyle

Worship is not so much what we *do*, but what we *are*. We are not called to *do* worship, but to *be* worshippers. To worship God is to be preoccupied with Him and become more like Him. Paul, in 2 Corinthians 3:18, says: 'And we, who with unveiled faces all reflect the Lord's glory, are being transformed into his likeness with ever-increasing glory, which comes from the Lord, who is the Spirit.' Rick Warren points out that 'Worship is far more than praising, singing, and praying to God. Worship is a lifestyle of *enjoying* God, *loving* him, and *giving* ourselves to be used for his purposes. When you use your life for God's glory, everything you do can become an act of worship.'[3]

In New Testament Greek, one word used for worship is *proskune* – to reverence towards and to kiss. The Anglo-Saxon expression is 'worth ship', to value. Do you have that level of intimacy with God and is it evident in all areas of your life and in all situations?

Surrender in the area of worship is about our worshipping God at all times, in all places, in all situations. The challenge is for us to reach a place where our *whole life* becomes an act of worship to the Lord, rather than worship being something that we do for a given period of time on a given day, because as someone once said, 'Worshipping God should be a full-time experience'.[4]

If we are honest, we are probably somewhat fickle in our worship or, as Dave Branon challenges us, 'Sometimes we worship Jesus heartily on Sunday, but the very next day we live as if we find His presence intrusive.'[5] In fact, as he rightly says, we are sadly little different from some of the crowd in Jesus' day who on Palm Sunday praised, honoured and cheered Jesus as He entered the city riding on a donkey (Matt. 21:6–11) and a few days later called for His crucifixion (Matt. 27:20–23).

If we are to free ourselves from acting in similar ways to the crowd, we must continue our journey of surrender. It is easy to assume that our worship is an area that is straightforward to surrender; that it is just a matter of giving greater time and focus to God. However, surrendering our worship involves examining and letting go of those things in our lives that have taken the place of God and which, to a greater or lesser degree, we worship. When we worship something we become preoccupied with the object of our worship. What are you preoccupied with and what or who is the object of your worship: self, money, possessions, TV, sport, fashion, husband/ wife, boyfriend/girlfriend, film star, body image? When God is the object of our worship it should be evident to non-believers that we have something far more worthwhile worshipping than they do!

## Captivating God's heart

God longs for our worship. Not only does God *long* for our worship but He is *worthy* of our worship. We worship God simply because He is *God*. He doesn't need a reason for us to worship Him; but *we* frequently do! In the times when we find it more difficult to worship God, it is good to remind ourselves of what He is like. The psalmist declares, '… how majestic is your name in all the earth' (Psa. 8:1). The Hebrew adjective for majestic is *addîyr* which, amongst other things, means powerful, glorious, mighty, stately, and distinguished. When *you* worship God, do you declare that He is powerful, glorious, mighty, stately, and distinguished?

Other characteristics to worship God for include: His splendour/excellence which is above the earth and the heavens (Psa. 148:13), His greatness which no one can fathom (Psa. 145:3), His wisdom and power (Dan. 2:20), His strength and might (Psa. 21:13) and His unfailing love and wonderful deeds (Psa. 107:8).

Worship encompasses all of our life, but perhaps it is the worship of the Lord through our voice, particularly singing, with which we are most familiar. It is important to surrender our voices and our acts of worship through song since we can so easily carry out this component of worship without engaging fully with God. I have all too frequently caught myself listening to the sound of my own voice, concentrating on other people's voices or looking around the room to see who else is there. Perhaps you have too. More recently I have had a real sense of conviction that when my mind drifts onto things other than God I am actually disengaging and no longer worshipping Him.

Something else that has come out of the process of surrendering my worship has been a greater awareness of the words that I am saying and whether my life reflects what I am singing. We sing words such as, 'I give you all of my life/honour/ glory etc ...' but do we in practice? Joe King, when leading a day on worship where I work, said, 'Unless worship changes us, it's not worship – it's just songs. God wants our worship to be living and our living to be worship ... We need not to just sing a song but come into the message of the truth of what we are singing.' How true and how we need to be transformed.

## A sweet aroma

In the tabernacle, the priests dropped incense on hot coals and a sweet aroma went up to the Lord (Exod. 30:1–10). Perhaps we need to ask ourselves how hot our worship is. Does it tend to become dampened down by lack of focus and repetitive singing or thinking more about the tune than connecting with God? If the coals aren't hot, the aroma doesn't go up; if we just sing songs but do not mean what we sing and our spirit does not engage with the Spirit of the Lord, then is this not similar to incense being dropped on tepid coals?

Out of the teachings about the tabernacle we also learn that it's important to be consistent in our worship: 'He must burn incense again ... so that incense will burn regularly before the LORD ...' (Exod. 30:8). Burning incense regularly is about being consistent. Perhaps we need to consider whether we are consistent in our worship. Do you have days when you worship God and days when you don't? Does your lifestyle match your worship?

For us to change we need to allow the Word of God to dwell in us and we need to be accountable to one another. In Colossians 3, Paul says, 'Let the word of Christ dwell in you richly as you teach and admonish one another with all wisdom, and as you sing psalms, hymns and spiritual songs with gratitude in your hearts to God' (v.16). Interestingly, Paul's words come under a section on 'Rules for Holy Living'. Does living a holy life not require us to be both obedient in our worship of God (Jesus' first commandment, 'Love the Lord your God with all your heart …') and obedient in our blessing of others (His second commandment, 'Love your neighbour as yourself' – see Mark 12:30–31)?

As we continue on the journey of surrender, may it not only bless us but may we be a blessing to others.

# For reflection

**Scriptures**

'... *I will sing to the* LORD, *for he is highly exalted.*'
(Exod. 15:1)

'*ascribe to the* LORD *the glory due to his name. Bring an offering and come before him; worship the* LORD *in the splendour of his holiness.*' (1 Chron. 16:29)

**Thought**

For a healthy spiritual life, our spirit needs to worship God in the same way that our body requires food and water in order to maintain our physical well-being.

**Action**

Think of the different ways and different times that you can worship God: listening to worship music and engaging in the words, walking in the country and worshipping the Creator for His creation; reflecting on His awesome power to change people's lives etc.

**Prayer**

*Lord! I give you my voice! May it proclaim Your might, Your power, Your majesty, and may it honour You. Help me to worship You in spirit and truth. Amen.*

## Chapter 10

# Reap the rewards

'… *whoever loses his life for me will find it.*'
Matthew 16:25

In my Introduction I spoke of how the thought of surrendering aspects of my life seemed like hard work. However, my way of looking at surrender in all its fullness is now significantly different. I have discovered that what I receive out of *letting go* of my life is far greater than what I could ever have found in *holding on* to it. What about you?

As you consider your response to what I have written, and before I conclude the book, perhaps it would be helpful to remind yourself of some of the key points we have looked at:

### Embrace surrender

- If we are to move from *following* Jesus to *living for* Jesus, and if we are to find freedom in all areas of our lives, then we need to embrace surrender.
- In order to surrender we must be convinced that surrender is positive, not negative, and we must rid ourselves of the viewpoint that it is a sign of weakness.
- Surrender, in biblical terms, means that we become fully God's and not our own; that we relinquish possession or control to God and give ourselves over to Him.
- The *granting* of our desires begins with the *surrender* of our desires.
- To surrender and allow God to be Lord of our lives involves not only a letting go but a belief that God directs our lives.
- To embrace surrender means examining our walk with God on a regular basis.
- Surrender involves a coming to the end of ourselves; letting that which is of ourselves die, in order that God-breathed life can emerge in us and bear fruit.
- Putting our confidence and trust in God and surrendering our lives to Him will bring greater fruitfulness.

## Soften your heart

- An un-surrendered heart can lead to internal and external chaos.
- We may genuinely love the Lord and yet, to our shame, still have ungodly attitudes and actions.
- It is often when we are at our lowest ebb and faced with our gravest mistakes that we are most open to God challenging, softening and remoulding our hearts.
- In order to soften and change our hearts we need to a) see God's heart for us and b) draw aside in order that He can change our hearts.
- Once we know God's heart for us it becomes easier to draw aside and allow Him to work on *our* hearts.
- We need to find a place of solitude where *our hearts* can meet with the *heart of God.*
- In our time of drawing aside it is helpful to look at whether there is any resistance in us to giving God the whole of our hearts and allowing Him to shape them.
- When our hearts have been softened and are malleable, the process of change becomes quicker and easier and we are more able to surrender the different areas of our lives.
- A heart surrendered by us and transformed by the Lord enables us to conduct our lives in a way pleasing to Him.

## Relinquish your will

- In contrast to our natural instinct to hold on to self, Jesus teaches us about laying self down.
- The danger is that if we do not surrender our will but go on choosing our own way we will end up battling with the consequences of our independence.
- To surrender our will to God means loving Him and being prepared to let go and allow our will to be shaped by Him.

- Surrendering our will can often be preceded by a coming to terms with the death of our own will and perhaps a time of grief and even disappointment.
- God can do more with our lives than we could ever attempt to.
- When we believe that God's will is so much better than ours it becomes easier to surrender.
- God longs to bless us in fulfilling His will for our lives even if at present we are puzzled over its outworking.
- Surrender is a *giving over* not a *giving up*. If we give up, we drown. If we give over, we move on.

## Commit your mind
- The longer we leave our minds unchallenged the more out of line our thinking becomes. The danger is that if left too long we get used to things being out of focus and this becomes our norm.
- Most of us live with thought patterns and minds that have the tendency to weaken rather than strengthen our walk with God.
- How we think affects the way we feel, the choices we make and to what extent we pursue our relationship with God.
- God yearns for us to recognise and respond to our need for a renewed mind, but we have the tendency to stray away from the truth and allow destructive thinking to take root.
- The mind is one area that Satan loves to attack and we tend to underestimate how destructive the enemy can be and how we can so easily be pulled into that destruction.
- To win that battle we need to understand what is happening in our minds, take our stand against the devil's schemes and become aware of the power of Christ to defeat the hold of the enemy.
- An important part of our minds being renewed is asking God to bind our mind to the mind of Christ.

**Offer your body**
- We are called to offer our bodies as living sacrifices, holy and pleasing to God.
- We are to care for our bodies, but not worship them, and we are to aspire to holiness of conduct, not perfection of the material.
- For our bodies to be holy and pleasing to the Lord we need to evaluate our health, eating habits, exercise levels, sleep patterns and stress levels.
- If our bodies are to be used by God, we need to take care of them as we would take care of Jesus if He Himself were with us in body.
- The Holy Spirit lives in us and as we reach out and touch the life of another we are actually taking Jesus to that person.
- God can use any part of us to impact the life of another: our words, smile, eyes and ability to listen.
- It is important to be willing to allow God to knock off our rough edges and to submit our weaknesses to Him.
- When we surrender our bodies, we are, in effect, saying to God, 'Use me in the way that You see best.'

**Hand over your time**
- Surrendering time often leads to a cleaning-up process as God reorders and prioritises how we use our moments.
- If we trust God with our moments then He will give back to us more than we have given up.
- Making the most of our time is about allowing the moments to matter and ensuring that they are handed over to God.
- By surrendering our time we are, effectively, asking God to lead us and guide us in our use of time and what it consists of.
- Surrendering our moments brings with it a whole new way of living and a completely different way of looking at life.
- Surrendering our moments requires us to put the direction,

the content and timing of our day into God's hands.

- When we surrender our time we are trusting that God will use our time for His purposes.
- Often we attempt to give over our moments and yet at the same time still stay in control. In reality we cannot do both successfully.

## Choose your words

- We must be mindful of the manner and content of our speech.
- The consequence of ungodly talk is that we will be led into further ungodliness (lack of reverence and a neglect of duty towards God, our neighbour and ourselves).
- Many of us tend to underestimate the power of our words, their effects upon others and the right we give to the enemy to cause disruption in our lives through what we say and the attitudes we hold.
- Our tongues have the power of life and death and the words we speak about others or ourselves result in purposefulness or destruction.
- Surrender of our words includes surrender of our tone of voice and body language.
- Besides our words we need to surrender our thoughts, which are words spoken internally.
- That which our lips, mouths and words utter, our lives must reflect and not contradict.

## Expand your love

- The love of Christ is a radiating love that flows out to others, not a love that feeds self; in contrast un-surrendered love has the tendency to consume or want something in return.
- If we want to expand our love we must spend time receiving God's love.

- God's love still flows out to us in abundance even though we look away from Him with eyes that wander towards the world, seeking earthly pleasure and self-gratification.
- If we do not seek after God with all our heart and in so doing discover the depth of His love for us it can be easy to deviate into seeking happiness in the form of conditional love.
- Without the certainty of God's unconditional love for us and our expression of love for Him we can end up manoeuvring our world in order to feel safe, and in so doing fail to relate to God and others in a way that brings satisfaction.
- When we seek after God with all our heart and spend time in His presence, His love flows in abundance, and we are more able to love both others and ourselves.
- God's love and acceptance of us as we are, despite our failings, lays the foundation for us to love and accept ourselves.
- As we love others with the love which Jesus has given us, we draw them closer to His love.

**Live out your worship**
- To live out our worship is to give God all aspects of our self in worship (heart, will, mind, body, time, words, love).
- If we can give God our soul, our life, our all, then our worship will be taken into a new dimension; as will our praise, since praise and worship are so closely linked.
- Worship is not so much what we *do*, but what we *are*. We are not called to *do* worship, but to *be* worshippers.
- To worship God is to be preoccupied with Him and become more like Him.
- Surrender in the area of worship is about our worshipping God at all times, in all places, in all situations; where our whole life becomes an act of worship to the Lord.
- Surrendering our worship involves examining and letting go

of those things in our lives that have taken the place of God and which, to a greater or lesser degree, we worship.

- Not only does God *long* for our worship but He is *worthy* of our worship.
- It is important to surrender our voices and our acts of worship through song since we can so easily carry out this component of worship without engaging fully with God.

## Go on practising

The Lord makes the most of what is unreservedly surrendered to Him: whatever we give Him, He will use. Not only will He make the most out of whatever we give Him but He will take our lives beyond where we can take them.

The benefits of journeying deeper with God and moving from what we could describe as *faith* to *living faith* (and deeper still, *sacrificial faith*) are clear. As we soak up the very nature of God and surrender to Him, His love inflames us and we become aware of how much He gives us. Amongst many other things, Scripture tells us that the Lord watches over us (Psa. 145:20), rescues us, protects us, answers us, delivers us, honours us (Psa. 91:14–15), makes His home with us (John 14:23) and brings about security (Heb. 6:19).

The danger is that in sharing our passion to surrender more of ourselves to God we can simplify the process and make it sound as though surrender itself is a one-off easy choice. Far from it; surrender is exactly what I have said, a process. The process is not dissimilar to salvation where we make the crucial decision to give our lives to Jesus and are saved, but are also called to continue to work out our salvation with fear and trembling (Phil. 2:12). To work out one's salvation is 'not a reference to earn one's salvation by works, but to the expression of one's salvation in spiritual growth and development. Salvation is not merely a gift received once for all; it expresses itself in an ongoing process in which the believer is strenuously involved'.[1]

As with salvation, surrender has a duel element to it, as Rick Warren points out: 'There is a *moment* of surrender, and there is the *practice* of surrender, which is moment-by-moment and lifelong. The problem with a *living* sacrifice is that it can crawl off the altar, so you may have to resurrender your life fifty times a day. You must make it a daily habit'.[2]

## Deep satisfaction

As we go on surrendering we cannot fail but to be blessed. I wonder what blessings you have so far encountered. Some of the ways in which I find I have been blessed are:

- an even deeper relationship with God
- a sense of time being extended
- an increased inner peace and security
- a confidence in God taking care of my needs
- more rewarding relationships with others
- an extended ability to hear God
- a clarity of direction in my life
- greater emotional and spiritual freedom.

The temptation when we begin to see the blessings is to want to do something, such as spend more time with God or verbally say that we are surrendering an area of our lives (even if our hearts are not ready) in order to enjoy the blessing. No, we do not surrender for the sake of surrender, because we want to be seen to be doing the right thing or because we desire the fruit of surrender, we surrender in response to our *love for God*. In other words, we do not surrender *in order* to be blessed; we are blessed *as a result* of our acts of surrender, and those acts of surrender are, inevitably, costly.

I have used the word blessed to describe the outcome of surrender, but as is the case with much 'Christian talk' it is not always obvious what we mean by the words we use. In New Testament Greek, the word *eulogeō* is sometimes used to translate 'blessed' which, amongst other things, means to cause to prosper and to make happy. Certainly the blessings we receive as a result of surrender lead to spiritual and emotional prosperity and joy.

Another Greek word for blessed is *makarioi*, which essentially means to be characterised by the quality of God. It indicates an indwelling by the nature and kingdom of God and it is something that is progressive. To be blessed also means to be *fully satisfied*. Words used to describe satisfaction include: gratification, comfort, delight, joy, pleasure, happiness, fulfilment, contentment.[3] 'The Bible is crystal clear how you benefit when you fully surrender your life to God. First you experience peace … Next you experience freedom … Third, you experience God's power in your life.'[4]

As we surrender and let go, we take up Jesus' invitation: 'Come to me, all you who are weary and burdened, and I will give you rest. Take my yoke upon you and learn from me, for I am gentle and humble in heart, and you will find rest for your souls. For my yoke is easy and my burden is light' (Matt. 11:28–29). To give Jesus all aspects of our lives, and live with the reality that He has them safe in His care, is a reflection of our finding freedom because we no longer carry burdens that do not belong to us. My prayer for you and for me is that we will make surrender a daily habit and we will go on growing in our relationship with God, discovering greater freedom and leading others in all truth.

## For reflection

### Scriptures
' ... *whoever loses his life for me will find it.*' (Matt. 16:25)

'*The eternal God is your refuge, and underneath are the everlasting arms.*' (Deut. 33:27)

### Thought
We are children of God and that cannot change, but what *can* change is whether we are victorious or defeated children of God. Without surrender we have the tendency to stumble through life blindly trying to manage by ourselves when, in fact, God has provided us with a comforter, guide and counsellor – the Holy Spirit – who will guide us into all truth (John 16:13).

### Action
As we draw our reflections to a close, spend a little while with the Lord considering the aspects of yourself which still require surrender and pray either 'change' my, 'take' my or 'use' my life; heart, will, mind, body, time, words, love, worship etc.

### Prayer
*Thank You, Lord, that You are changing me and I am witnessing greater freedom and joy in my life. Help me to continue to surrender more and more of myself to You so that I clearly reflect Jesus in my life. Amen.*

# Notes

## Chapter 1

1. 'I Surrender All' by Judson W. Van Deventer, 1847–1908.
2. Rick Warren, *The Purpose Driven Life* (Grand Rapids, Michigan, USA: Zondervan, 2002), p.77.
3. *Reader's Digest Universal Dictionary* (London, UK: The Reader's Digest Association Ltd., 1986), p.1524.
4. *Reader's Digest Oxford Complete Wordfinder* (London, UK: The Reader's Digest Association Ltd., 1990), p.1572.
5. Ibid., p.285.
6. *Reader's Digest Universal Dictionary*, op. cit., p.322.
7. *The Word for Today* (PO Box 255, Stoke-on-Trent, ST4 8YY: UCB, 2006). Extract: 10 January 2006. (Free issues of the daily devotional are available for the UK and Republic of Ireland.)
8. Rick Warren, *The Purpose Driven Life*, op. cit., p.78.
9. *Reader's Digest Oxford Complete Wordfinder*, op. cit., p.1676.

## Chapter 2

1. Edward Sanford Martin (1856–1939), taken from James Dalton Morrison (ed.) 'My Name is Legion' in *Masterpieces of Religious Verse* (New York: Harper, 1948), p.274.
2. *Reader's Digest Oxford Complete Wordfinder*, op. cit., p.791.
3. *Reader's Digest Universal Dictionary* (London, UK: The Reader's Digest Association Ltd., 1986) p.799.

## Chapter 3

1. Rick Warren, *The Purpose Driven Life*, op. cit., p.83.

## Chapter 4

1. W. Backus and M. Chapian, *Telling Yourself the Truth* (Minneapolis: Bethany House, 1980), p.35.
2. Neil T. Anderson and Dave Park, *Stomping out the Darkness* (California, USA: Regal Books, 1993), pp.140–142.
3. Selwyn Hughes, *Every Day with Jesus, The Mind of The Christian* (Farnham, Surrey, UK: CWR, September/October 1994). Extract: 31 October 1994.

## Chapter 5

1. Matthew Henry's *Commentary on the Whole Bible* (Basingstoke: Marshall Pickering, 1960), p.582.
2. 2001 © Jan Sutch Pickard from *Lent & Easter Readings from Iona* http://www.ionabooks.com. Used by permission.

## Chapter 6

1. Mart De Haan, *Our Daily Bread* (Grand Rapids, Michigan, USA: RBC Ministries). Extract: 1 June 2007.
2. Anne Morrow Lindbergh, quoted in *365 Day Brighteners, for Women by Women* (Siloam Springs, Arkansas, USA: Garborg's™, DaySpring Cards Inc., 2003) 18 November 2003.

## Chapter 7

1. Ray Prichard, *The ABC's of Wisdom* (Chicago, USA: Moody Press, 1997), pp.128–129.
2. Ibid., p.129.

## Chapter 8

1. David Roper, *Our Daily Bread*, op. cit. Extract: 26 October 2006.
2. Selwyn Hughes, *Every Day with Jesus, The Fruit of the Spirit* (Farnham, Surrey, UK: CWR, May/June 1987). Extract: 7 May 1987.
3. John Powell, S.J., *Unconditional Love* (Allen, TX, Valencia, CA, USA: Tabor Publishing, 1978), p.78.

## Chapter 9

1. Rick Warren, *The Purpose Driven Life*, op. cit., p.77.
2. *Our Daily Bread*, op. cit. Extract: 20 September 2006.
3. Rick Warren, *The Purpose Driven Life*, op. cit., p.56.
4. Dave Branon, *Our Daily Bread*, op. cit., Extract: 5 April 2007.
5. Ibid.

## Chapter 10

1. Commentary in the *NIV Study Bible* (London, UK: Hodder & Stoughton, 1987), p.1772.
2. Rick Warren, *The Purpose Driven Life*, op. cit., pp.83–84.
3. *Reader's Digest Oxford Complete Wordfinder*, 1990, op. cit., p.1368.
4. Rick Warren, *The Purpose Driven Life*, op. cit., p.82.

---

## Other books by Helena Wilkinson

*Puppet on a String* (Horsham, UK: first published Hodder & Stoughton, 1984; RoperPenberthy Publishing, 2004).

*Snakes and Ladders* (Horsham, UK: first published Hodder & Stoughton, 1988; RoperPenberthy Publishing, 2007).

*Beyond Chaotic Eating* (First published Harper Collins, 1993; RoperPenberthy Publishing, 2001).

*Beyond Singleness* (First published Harper Collins, 1995; RoperPenberthy Publishing, 2004.)

*Breaking Free from Loneliness* (First published Harper Collins 1997; RoperPenberthy Publishing, 2004).

*A Way Out of Despair* (Farnham, Surrey, UK: CWR, 1995).

*Insight into Eating Disorders* (Farnham, Surrey, UK: CWR, 2006).

**Website:** www.helenawilkinson.co.uk

# National Distributors

**UK: (and countries not listed below)**
CWR, Waverley Abbey House, Waverley Lane, Farnham, Surrey GU9 8EP.
Tel: (01252) 784700 Outside UK (44) 1252 784700

**AUSTRALIA:** CMC Australasia, PO Box 519, Belmont, Victoria 3216.
Tel: (03) 5241 3288 Fax: (03) 5241 3290

**CANADA:** Cook Communications Ministries, PO Box 98, 55 Woodslee Avenue, Paris, Ontario N3L 3E5.
Tel: 1800 263 2664

**GHANA:** Challenge Enterprises of Ghana, PO Box 5723, Accra.
Tel: (021) 222437/223249 Fax: (021) 226227

**HONG KONG:** Cross Communications Ltd, 1/F, 562A Nathan Road, Kowloon.
Tel: 2780 1188 Fax: 2770 6229

**INDIA:** Crystal Communications, 10-3-18/4/1, East Marredpalli, Secunderabad – 500026, Andhra Pradesh.
Tel/Fax: (040) 27737145

**KENYA:** Keswick Books and Gifts Ltd, PO Box 10242, Nairobi. Tel: (02) 331692/226047
Fax: (02) 728557

**MALAYSIA:** Salvation Book Centre (M) Sdn Bhd, 23 Jalan SS 2/64, 47300 Petaling Jaya, Selangor.
Tel: (03) 78766411/78766797  Fax: (03) 78757066/78756360

**NEW ZEALAND:** CMC Australasia, PO Box 303298, North Harbour, Auckland 0751.
Tel: 0800 449 408 Fax: 0800 449 049

**NIGERIA:** FBFM, Helen Baugh House, 96 St Finbarr's College Road, Akoka, Lagos.
Tel: (01) 7747429/4700218/825775/827264

**PHILIPPINES:** OMF Literature Inc, 776 Boni Avenue, Mandaluyong City.
Tel: (02) 531 2183 Fax: (02) 531 1960

**SINGAPORE:** Alby Commercial Enterprises Pte Ltd, 95 Kallang Avenue #04-00, AIS Industrial Building, 339420.
Tel: (65) 629 27238 Fax: (65) 629 27235

**SOUTH AFRICA:** Struik Christian Books, 80 MacKenzie Street, PO Box 1144, Cape Town 8000.
Tel: (021) 462 4360 Fax: (021) 461 3612

**SRI LANKA:** Christombu Publications (Pvt) Ltd, Bartleet House, 65 Braybrooke Place, Colombo 2.
Tel: (9411) 2421073/2447665

**TANZANIA:** CLC Christian Book Centre, PO Box 1384, Mkwepu Street, Dar es Salaam.
Tel/Fax: (022) 2119439

**USA:** Cook Communications Ministries, PO Box 98, 55 Woodslee Avenue, Paris, Ontario N3L 3E5, Canada.
Tel: 1800 263 2664

**ZIMBABWE:** Word of Life Books (Pvt) Ltd, Christian Media Centre, 8 Aberdeen Road, Avondale, PO Box A480
Avondale, Harare.  Tel: (04) 333355 or 091301188

**For email addresses, visit the CWR website: www.cwr.org.uk**

**CWR is a Registered Charity – Number 294387**

**CWR is a Limited Company registered in England – Registration Number 1990308**

Day and Residential Courses
Counselling Training
Leadership Development
Biblical Study Courses
Regional Seminars
Ministry to Women
Daily Devotionals
Books and Videos
Conference Centre

# Trusted all Over the World

CWR HAS GAINED A WORLDWIDE reputation as a centre of excellence for Bible-based training and resources. From our headquarters at Waverley Abbey House, Farnham, England, we have been serving God's people for over 40 years with a vision to help apply God's Word to everyday life and relationships. The daily devotional *Every Day with Jesus* is read by nearly a million readers an issue in more than 150 countries, and our unique courses in biblical studies and pastoral care are respected all over the world. Waverley Abbey House provides a conference centre in a tranquil setting.

**For free brochures** on our seminars and courses, conference facilities, or a catalogue of CWR resources, please contact us at the following address.
CWR, Waverley Abbey House, Waverley Lane, Farnham, Surrey GU9 8EP, UK

Telephone: +44 (0)1252 784700
Email: mail@cwr.org.uk
Website: www.cwr.org.uk

**CWR** Applying God's Word
*to everyday life and relationships*

## Inspiring Women: Created as a Woman

Beverley Shepherd takes a fresh look at what it means
to be a woman, drawing from biblical insights, personal
testimonies and her own life experiences. Following the
themes of creation, the Fall, redemption, being chosen,
transformation and glory, Beverley challenges us with
searching questions and tells us that every woman can
know the Lord's total, unconditional, unchangeable and
eternal love.

£6.99
ISBN: 978-1-85345-450-9

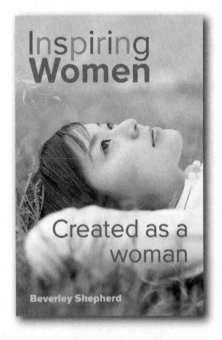